THE WOMAN IN BATTLE:

A NARRATIVE OF THE

Exploits & Adventures

OF

A Woman Officer

in the

Confederate Army

Loreta Velazquez

OTHERWISE KNOWN AS

LIEUTENANT HARRY T. BUFORD,

CONFEDERATE STATES ARMY

Full Descriptions of the numerous Battles in which she
participated as a Confederate Officer; of her Perilous
Performances as a Spy, as a Bearer of Despatches,
as a Secret-Service Agent, and as a Blockade-Runner; of her Adventures Behind the Scenes at
Washington, &c., faithfully attenuated
from her rare publication of 1878.

Profusely Illustrated by
Alan Archambault

Loreta dreams of being a heroine like Joan of Arc.

Chapter One

From my earliest childhood, Joan of Arc was my favorite heroine. A religious enthusiast as well as a born leader of men and a martial genius of the first order, this great woman infused courage and determination into the heart of a weak and cowardly king. Seizing the banner of France, she rallied, defeated and demoralized armies and led them with terrible effect against the British foe.

Many a time has my soul burned with an overwhelming desire to emulate her deeds of valor and make for myself a name which would be enrolled in letters of gold among the women who had the courage to fight like men—nay, better than most men—for a great cause.

At length an opportunity arose, in the conflict between the North and South in 1861, for me to carry out my long-cherished ideas. I embraced it with an impetuous eagerness, combined with a calm determination, to see the thing through and to shrink from nothing such a step would involve.

I have every reason to be proud of the name I bear. My father's family is an ancient one connected with some of the most impressive episodes of Spanish history. Don Diego Velazquez, the conqueror and first governor of Cuba, was one of my ancestors, and Don Diego Rodriguez Velazquez, the greatest artist that Spain ever produced, was a member of my family. I came of excellent—although somewhat fiery and headstrong—stock.

My father was a native of the city of Carthagena; an accomplished Latin, French and German scholar and a very strict Catholic. He went to Paris as an attach of the Spanish embassy. My mother was the daughter of a French naval officer by an American lady, the daughter of a wealthy merchant. My father's marriage occurred a short time before his recall to Spain, where three sons and two daughters were born.

In 1840 my father was appointed to a position in Cuba and two years later I came into the world in a house on the Calle Velaggas near the walls of Havana. When I was almost one my father inherited a large estate in Texas, which was then a part of Mexico. He resigned his position in Cuba in 1844 and moved our family to Central Mexico. We had scarcely settled in our new house when the war between Mexico and the United States broke out. My father received a commission in the army and took to the field against the United States. During the conflict his estates and his property were destroyed and this greatly embittered him against the Americans.

When the war was brought to an end, and a large portion of Northern Mexico ceded to the United States, my father refused to live under a government he disliked so intensely. In the meantime he had inherited another valuable estate at Puerto de Palmas [in Cuba]. Settling upon it, he engaged actively in the sugar, tobacco and coffee trade and speedily acquired great wealth.

While we were residing on the Puerto de Palmas plantation, an English goveness was employed to conduct my education. I remained under this good lady's instruction until 1849, acquiring a fair knowledge of the English language. In that year, my father determined to send me to New Orleans. I took up residence with my mother's only surviving sister. My aunt was rather strict with me, but she took great pains with my education. Having become reasonably proficient in such studies as were assigned by my aunt, I was

Loreta tries on her cousin's clothing.

sent to the school conducted by the Sisters of Charity to learn the ornamental branches.

I was especially haunted with the idea of being a man. While residing with my aunt it was frequently my habit, after all of the house had retired to bed at night, to dress myself in my cousin's clothes and promenade by the hour before the mirror, practicing the gait of a man and admiring the figure I made in masculine raiment. I wished that I could change places with my brother. If I could have, I would have marked out for myself a military career, and have disported myself in the gay uniform of an officer.

Some time before my admission to school, I was betrothed to a young Spaniard, Raphael R., in accordance with plans which my relatives had formed without any action on my part. Indeed, my consent was not asked, my parents thinking that they were much better qualified to arrange a suitable alliance than I was and that love was something of minor importance that could very well be left to take care of itself.

This does not seem to be the proper way of conducting such an important piece of business as marriage, and it is very contrary to the notions which are common in the United States. I had not been long in the school when I learned that it was not considered correct for parents of a young lady to pick out a husband for her. The girls were at great pains to inform me that this was a free country and that a girl could not be compelled to marry if she did not choose to do so.

This kind of talk excited me and I began to wish to break my engagement with Raphael. Such a course as this, however, I knew would sever me from my family; and as I had the fondest regard for my dear father and mother, I took no steps to get rid of Raphael until I chanced to make the acquaintance of a young American army officer who was paying particular attention to my roommate Nellie V. He was a handsome young officer and his manly appearance, especially when attired in his brilliant uniform, made such an impression on my heart that I could soon think of nothing else.

I learned to hate Raphael. His attempts to make himself agreeable only served to increase my dislike. I soon became savagely jealous of Nellie. At length I became desperate and determined to acquaint the young officer with the affection I entertained for him. One evening Nellie and I agreed to exchange partners for the purpose of finding out how much they loved us. Finding that I had not the courage to speak, I wrote a few words in his pocket diary which told him everything.

When my lover began to appear at my aunt's as a pretty constant visitor, Raphael became furiously jealous and prevailed upon my aunt to forbid him admittance to the house. In spite of my aunt's endeavors to keep us apart, William—for that was my lover's name—found means to speak to me on my way to and from school. I was threatened with being locked up in a convent or sent back to Cuba if I did not conduct myself with more propriety.

My lover informed me that he expected to be ordered to one of the frontier posts and proposed that we should elope and get married secretly. I told him that I would prefer he make an open proposition for my hand to my parents. William wrote to my father and asked his permission to marry me. A reply to his letter was not long forthcoming. William was reprimanded in very harsh terms for daring to make such a proposition. This settled the matter: on the fifth of April, 1856 we were clandestinely married.

This was a terrible blow to my aunt, but an even greater one to my parents, especially to my father, who idolized me. He promptly informed me that I was to consider

Loreta meets William.

myself repudiated and disinherited. My separation from my family caused me much grief, but I tried not to let my husband see how I suffered. I entered as far as possible into his thoughts and wishes and gratified a natural taste by giving a large portion of my time to the study of military tactics.

I longed for war to break out and resolved that I would follow my husband to the battlefield and minister to him, even if I was not allowed to fight by his side.

Chapter Two

In 1857 there appeared to be a chance that my martial aspirations would be gratified. The government organized an expedition against the Mormons, and my husband was ordered to accompany it. In the meantime, however, I had become a mother; much as I desired to accompany the army to Utah, I was forced to acknowledge the impracticability of a journey across the plains with an infant in my arms.

When my baby came into the world, I yearned more than ever to be reconciled with my family. With my husband's consent, I wrote to my mother and to my favorite brother. They worked so successfully on the feelings of my father that, after a somewhat stubborn resistance, he yielded. When I met him for the first time after my marriage, he turned his cheek to me saying, "You can never impress a kiss on my lips after a union with my country's enemy." It was not so much my marriage as my alliance with an American that embittered him.

After the Mormon expedition, my husband took me to Fort Leavenworth, a remote frontier town. I bore every discomfort and, over the course of time, became a good American. I was as happy as I could wish to be.

In the spring of 1860 I returned to St. Louis, while my husband went to Fort Arbuckle. During his separation from me, our third babe was born and died. In October, my two remaining children died of fever. My grief at their loss probably had a great influence in reviving my old notions about military glory and exciting anew my desire to win fame on the battlefield.

About this time, my husband received a summons that a war was about to break out between the North and the South. My husband's state determined to secede. It was a great grief for him to forsake the uniform he had worn so long with honor. He much doubted the wisdom of the Southern States in taking the action they did.

I was perfectly wild on the subject of war, and was busy night and day in planning schemes for making my name famous—above that of any of the great heroines of history, not even excepting Joan of Arc. I desired to obtain my husband's consent, but he would not listen to anything I had to say on the subject. My heart was set on accompanying him to war and I would listen to no other arrangement. He used every possible argument to dissuade me, contending that it would be impossible for him to permit his wife to follow an undisciplined army of volunteers. He was not to be persuaded, while I persisted in arguing the point with him to the last.

My husband thought he would be able to cure me of my erratic fancies. He permitted me to dress myself in one of his suits, and said he would take me to the barrooms and other places of male resort. Braiding my hair very close, I put on a man's wig and a false mustache. By tucking my pantaloons into my boots, as I had seen men do frequently, and otherwise arranging my garments, I managed to transform myself into a very presentable man. I fancied that I made quite as good-looking a man as my husband. We crossed over to a barroom filled with men smoking and drinking, and doing some pretty tall talking about the war. Every man present was full of fight and was burning with a furious desire to meet the enemy. A good many men will say things over a glass of whiskey in a barroom who won't do a tenth of what they say once they are within smelling distance of gunpowder.

My husband caught sight of a couple of men who had belonged to his regiment, and who were particular friends of mine. I was dreadfully afraid they would recognize me. I took a glass of sarsaparilla, and raising my tumbler, cried out, "Gentlemen, here's to the success of our young Confederacy!" My heart was almost ready to jump out of my throat. The men gave a rousing cheer and yelled out, "We drink that toast every time, young fellow!"

I was glad to get out of the barroom, and when we were once more in our room, my husband said, "Well, don't you feel disgusted?"

To please him I said, "Yes," adding, however, "but then I can stand anything to be with you and to serve the sunny South."

"Now Loreta," said he, "What you have seen and heard is nothing to what you see and hear in camp. The language and the sights are simply indescribable."

I pretended to be satisfied with his arguments, but was resolved to put my plans into action as soon as he took his departure. I waited impatiently for him to leave, intending to show him that his wife was as good as soldier as he.

My husband's farewell kisses were sarcely dry upon my lips when I ordered two uniform suits, for which I agreed to pay eighty-five dollars each. My coats were heavily padded in the back to disguise my shape. But the padding was uncomfortable, and I soon made up my mind that it would never do. As soon as I got to New Orleans, I went to an old tailor in Barrack Street and had him make for me half a dozen fine wire net shields. These I wore next to my skin, and they proved satisfactory in concealing my true form. With such underwear as I used, any woman who can disguise her features can readily pass for a man. Many a time I have gone to sleep when sixty officers have been lying close together in camp and have had no more fear of detection than I had of drinking a glass of water.

Within three days I managed to provide myself with a very complete military outfit. I had in mind to present myself before my husband so that he could no longer find an excuse for refusing his consent to my joining the Southern army as a soldier. I soon had in my room a trunk well packed with the wearing apparel of an army officer, and neatly marked upon the outside with the name I had concluded to adopt:

LIEUTENANT H. T. BUFORD, C.S.A.

When I saw the trunk with this name upon it I felt as if the dream of my life were already more than half realized. I thought and planned until my head fairly ached. I concluded to call in a gentleman who was a very old and intimate friend of both my husband and myself, and demand his assistance.

This friend turned deathly pale when I informed him of my intention to disguise myself as a man and to enter the army on exactly the same footing as other combatants. He believed I was either a little demented, or was indulging in an absurd bit of pleasantry. My friend thought it his duty to persuade me to abandon my wild ideas. He might as well have talked to the wind, for my heart was fixed on achieving fame and accomplishing even more than the great heroines of history. He finally promised to give his aid. He managed to get me into my new quarters without my being observed by anyone.

My friend retired and left me to myself. I proceeded to change my garments, and I was transformed into a man. He admitted that I should be able to credit the name I bore and the clothes I wore. The only regret I had was in parting with my long and luxuriant hair. There was no help for it, though. Before going to the barber's, he made me promenade the room, practicing my masculine gait. He enjoined me to watch his actions closely at the barber's, in the drinking saloons, and the billiard room for the purpose of informing me with masculine habits.

A carriage having been sent for, we were driven to an old Virginian negro barber, an obsequious colored individual, vigorously mixing lather in a cup. This he intended to apply to my face, notwithstanding that I had not the least sign of a beard. I was very much amused, but also frightened, for I did not want to have my face scraped with a razor. My friend came to the rescue, informing the barber that his young friend only wanted his hair trimmed in the latest style. The negro grinned a little, at which I was almost inclined to believe that he had suspicions. While he trimmed my hair he said, "De young gemmen in de military always likes to be shaved, sah, even if dey hasn't any beard. Dey tinks dat it helps to make de beard grow, sah." He laughed heartily at the expense of an important class of his customers. I appreciated the joke immensely, and assured my colored friend that I had no disposition to force my beard, but thought that it would come of itself in due time. It was evident that he took me for a young man. I was greatly reassured with my disguise, and left the shop with increased confidence.

My friend warned me that he was about to take me to places with which I would not be so well pleased, and in which I would be compelled to be constantly on my guard. We soon came to the hotel and entered the barroom. I was received with great cordiality. Of course, as soon as the first introductions were over, somebody suggested drinks. The men all took whiskey straight; but I did not venture on anything stronger than cider. I had never seen a game of billiards played before, and I became interested in watching in my shirt-sleeves, pretending to smoke my cigar, the balls rolling over the table.

I felt bound to do whatever my instructor in masculine manners desired of me. Entering a faro bank, my companion cautioned me not to take part in games like faro, or to drink any strong liquor. He said that I had better at once establish a reputation for temperance. Once it was understood that I never touched whiskey, brandy, or even wine, I could manage to get along very well with hard drinkers. My friend felt that even a slight indiscretion might get me into serious trouble and thwart my plans.

He recognized a number of acquaintances to whom he introduced me. A major eyed me pretty closely, and proposed that we drink. All but myself called for brandy. I took cider, whereupon the major said with a smile, "Lieutenant, you don't appear to be a heavy drinker."

"No," replied my friend, "he is quite temperate."

Lt. Buford receives a shave and a haircut.

Said the major, "Hard drinking is a bad habit." Then turning to me, he said, "What part of the country do you come from?"

"He has just returned from the North," put in my friend.

"I am glad to find him on the right side," said the major. "He is the kind of fellow we want."

In a few moments a dozen men gathered around, shaking my hand and plying me with questions. I informed them that it was my intention to recruit and equip a company at my own expense, and that I had eighty-eight thousand dollars with which to see myself through. The major proposed to show me the sights. I thanked him, but said it was very late. My friend seconded my efforts to get away, and we finally reached the house. It was after four o'clock when I went to sleep.

The next day I completed my outfit by purchasing a pair of field-glasses, a pair of blankets, a rubber overcoat, and a rubber blanket. I made out a form of attorney in my friend's name, and authorized him to attend to all my business matters for me.

My friend obtained for me a false mustache and a solution with which to stain my face. I rubbed on the solution and then my friend fastened the mustache on my upper lip with glue. I scarcely knew myself when I looked in the glass, and laughed at the thought of what my husband would say when he saw me in this disguise.

That day I received two letters: one from my father, informing me that he was about to return to Cuba, and the other postmarked from Vicksburg, from my husband. In my reply to the latter, I stated that I was going to Texas, for the purpose of accompanying my father to Cuba. This I thought would prevent my husband from being apprehensive and enable me to get matters under good headway. I was extremely anxious to give him a first-rate surprise.

Everything was now in proper trim for me to commence operations in earnest. I was ready to start on my campaign with as stout a heart as ever beat in the breast of a soldier.

Chapter Three

The plan of action I had fixed upon was to raise and equip a battalion at my own expense, to appear at the head of my little army before my husband, and to offer him the command. I flattered myself that, so far from being inclined to censure me for my persistence, he would praise my actions. Whatever view of the matter he might take, however, he would be compelled to yield to my wishes, and I would be free to follow my inclinations. My desire was to serve with him, but if this could not be done, I intended to play my part in the war in my own way. I started out on the war-path with a light heart and brilliant anticipations for the future.

I crossed over to Hopefield and took the five o'clock train. I busied myself with the study of my Manual of Tactics. Having been the wife of an army officer, I was pretty well qualified for the work I had now undertaken. I had paid attention to the details of military organizations and had seen soldiers drilled hundreds of times. Finding the conductor at leisure, I asked him if he could suggest a good neighborhood for me to commence operations. Hurlburt Station, he told me, was not much of a place - a saw mill, a country store, and a school house was all there was of it. Most of the young men thereabouts would, he thought, be glad to have a crack at the Yankees.

In accordance with the conductor's suggestion, I alighted at Hurlburt Station and made for the nearest house. A negro stared at me a bit, and then said that the young boss - Frank Giles - was about somewhere. I told him to call him. In response to my inquiry as to whether I could stop there for a few days, he said, "I guess so, if you can stand our fare."

As we entered the house, Frank bawled out at the top of his voice, "Mammy, here's a man who wants to stop here."

The old woman and the young fellow both stared at me with open-mouthed astonishment when they saw my uniform, and began to deluge me with questions. The sight of my brass buttons fired Frank with military ardor.

"I guess you're an officer, ain't you?" asked Frank. "What army do you belong to?"

"To the army of Virginia," I replied.

"Then I reckon you are for the South," said he.

"Certainly, sir," said I, "and you?"

The sudden intrusion of a gallant young officer, plentifully decorated with buttons and lace, made an even greater impression on the female part of the family. While making my toilet, I noticed the old woman and a couple of girls peeking at me through a crack in the wall. I, without appearing to notice them, took pains to strut about in as mannish a manner as I could. The eldest of the two daughters was about sixteen, the youngest was about twelve.

On entering the room, the old woman said, "These is my gals, sir."

I bowed and said, "Good evening, ladies," laying an emphasis on the word "ladies." The eldest simpered, as she heartily enjoyed it.

I said, "Madam, I am trying to enlist your son for a soldier; don't you think you can spare him?"

She burst out crying. The youngest girl began to blubber too, but the eldest did not cry. She looked at me in such a peculiar way that I was convinced she wished I would take her instead of Frank.

The idea of having a mild flirtation with this fair flower of the Arkansas forest grew upon me, and I had some curiosity to know how love-making went from the masculine standpoint. It occurred to me that if I was to figure successfully in the role of a dashing young Confederate officer, it would be necessary for me to learn how to make myself immensely agreeable to the ladies. My flirtation with Miss Sadie Giles was not a very savage one, and I hope that it did not inflict more damage on her heart than it did on mine. I commenced to ogle her and to pay her some delicate attentions. The heart which beat under her yellow calico dress was in a great state of excitement; Miss Sadie made it understood that my attentions were appreciated.

Before supper was over, I had a terrible fright. While drinking a glass of buttermilk, which was the best thing on the table, my mustache got full of the liquid. When I attempted to wipe it, I fancied that it was loose and about to fall off. I managed to keep a straight countenance, keeping my hand to my mouth all the time, and doing my best to hold the mustache on. After supper, I had a little time to myself. To my intense relief, I found it as fast as if it actually grew on my lip. With a light heart I returned to the girls.

After a variety of inquiries about the war, the old woman asked whether I had any parents. I replied that my father was living.

"Are you married?" was the next query.

"No, madam," I replied, giving a sharp look at Sadie.

"You are much better off, young man," struck in the old man Giles. Miss Sadie took a wooden stool, upon which she seated herself quite close to me. I asked her if there were any churches in the neighborhood.

Mr. Giles did not want any more conversation that night, so I excused myself and stepped out on the porch to think what I had best do next. That I could successfully pass myself off as a man with both sexes was a fact. I resolved to dare everything to make success a certainty. I got back to the room, threw myself on the bed, and fell into a deep and dreamless sleep.

The noise of the coffee-mill disturbed my slumbers in the morning. I jumped out of bed, thinking that laziness would never do if I intended to be a soldier. I was in a few moments seated by the side of Miss Sadie, who blushed furiously as I greeted her.

When breakfast was over, I crossed over to the schoolhouse where I found half a dozen rather rough fellows waiting to see me, extremely anxious to enlist. I encouraged them to believe that they all might be lieutenants, captains, and even generals, someday, if they fought bravely. I wrote out bills calling for volunteers, one of which I posted on the schoolhouse door. The rest I gave to Frank, who mounted a horse and started off to distribute them through the country. My quota was easily filled in four days. Two of the most intelligent of the men I appointed subordinate officers, giving them instructions about drilling the battalion and maintaining discipline in my absence.

I bid good-bye to the Giles family. The old man did not fancy losing both his boys, but he stood it bravely. The old woman broke down entirely. Both girls cried; Miss Sadie, I thought, more at the idea of parting with me than with losing her brothers.

My men were decidedly of the opinion that soldiering was harder work than they had calculated. I do not think any of them appreciated the real importance of what they were doing and looked upon the whole affair much in the light of an excursion which would be rather jolly than otherwise. I regarded the thing in that light myself, notwithstanding that I had seen enough of military life to understand its serious character.

At the landing I met my Memphis friend. He handed me a letter from my husband. This I eagerly read, and learned that he had gone to Pensacola. I determined to meet him there, for I was bent on offering him the command of my battalion. I embarked my men - two hundred and thirty-six in all - upon the steamer *Ohio Belle*, and issued blankets and other articles for their comfort.

On arriving in New Orleans, I purchased my commissary stores and perfected my private outfit. Among my other purchases was a fine horse. No finer body of men ever went out of New Orleans than the Arkansas Grays, as my battalion was called. As we passed through Mobile we were heartily cheered, the men waving their hats, and the women their handkerchiefs, and everybody commenting in the most laudatory terms upon our appearance. I cannot tell how proud I was. I felt that in spite of my being a woman, I was intended for military leadership, and resolved more firmly than ever to let nothing stand in the way of my winning the fame I coveted.

At Pensacola we were received by my husband, who had not the slightest idea who

Lt. Buford and the Arkansas Grays.

I was, and who would not have recognized me had I not revealed myself. As soon as I was able, I took him aside and disclosed my identity. He was greatly grieved and said he would not for the world have made me attempt such a thing. I told him I was determined to be a soldier. He was proud of the ability I had displayed in carrying out my plans, and seeing the uselessness of further argument, took command of my men.

I was ordered back to New Orleans to purchase more equipment. I had scarcely arrived at my destination when I received a dispatch announcing the death of my husband. Nearly wild with grief, I started for Pensacola and found that, while drilling his men, a weapon had exploded in his hands, killing him instantly.

Chapter Four

During the brief time I had been in Pensacola I had made the acquaintance of a number of officers who were going to the front. I concluded that it would be better to go in their company, especially as one or two of them were particular friends of my late husband. I also became acquainted with a good many ladies; one, a dashing young widow, paid my masculine charms the compliment of falling in love with them. I was rather shy, and she took pains to let me know the sentiments she felt for me.

I was in no mood for nonsense of this kind, and was not pleased with the unfeminine advances that were made toward me. The necessity of playing the character I had assumed, however, was requisite to divert my mind from my bereavement. I determined to meet my fair one half way, and paid her numerous attentions, such as taking her to the theatre, and to drive upon the beach. I resolutely refused to accept her very broad hints that more love-making would be agreeable.

I assured her that I had never courted a lady in my life and did not know how to begin. The widow undertook to instruct me, which was decidedly comical, and I learned more of the fine points of feminine nature from her in a week than I had picked up myself in twenty years. I had not imagined that it was possible for a lady to take such an important matter so entirely out of the gentleman's hands. I pretended to soften to her, and by the time I was ready to start for Virginia, we were the best possible friends. The widow parted from me with the understanding that when the war was over we were to be more than friends. Being a woman, this and other love adventures have a comical interest. If they do not show some members of my own sex in the best light, it is their fault and not mine.

On the sixteenth of June I started for Virginia with a jovial party of fellows who had a good deal of whiskey with them. I was constantly importuned to drink, my refusing to do so not having the best possible effect on some of them.. The conversation became profane and ribald. I was not only disgusted, but the warning I had received from my husband came into my mind, and had a most depressing influence on me. Much of the talk was meaningless blackguardism, and my ears were saluted for the first time with nastiness in the shape of language.

On the train north there was another quite jovial party, not so much addicted to whiskey drinking. A good deal of the conversation was about wives and sweethearts, and pictures of the loved ones at home were handed about. I was rallied rather severely because I could not show a photograph of my sweetheart.

Before the journey was ended, I had an opportunity to prove myself as good a lady's man as the best of them. On the train for Richmond, a gentleman asked if I could take charge of some ladies. I resolved to play the gallant, although my heart was in my throat and I could scarcely find the voice to announce myself as Lieutenant Buford.

We arrived at Richmond. Two of the ladies accompanied me to the Ballard House, where I obtained rooms for them. The youngest—a very pretty girl, who seemed to have taken quite a fancy to me—had the room adjoining mine. I had scarcely established myself in my quarters when a waiter handed me a card, asking me to escort her to supper. I dressed myself in my best apparel and after a visit to the barber I was ready to play the gallant.

I confess that my heart failed me when we entered the dining room. When the steward said, "Lieutenant, step this way with your lady," it seemed as if every eye in the room was fixed on me. I was conspicuous for my uniform, made of the best cloth and trimmed with buttons and gold lace, was calculated to attract attention.

My lady at length finished her supper. I hurried her out of the room as fast as I could, and repaired to the drawing room. I returned to the hotel at one o'clock in the morning. On going to my room, I found a note from my lady friend, requesting me to visit her in her chamber. This astonished me and assuredly did not increase my good opinion of her. I slept late the next morning, and found to my satisfaction that my lady had left before I was out of bed.

During the day I bought two horses, shipped them, and provided myself with a number of articles necessary for the campaign. The next morning I was off on the five o'clock train, anxious to to see what fighting really was.

Chapter Five

I was now about to see some real warfare, to engage in real battles, do some real fighting, and to have some opportunities for distinguishing myself. I was never in better health and spirits than on that bright summer morning when I left Richmond. I had only one fear: that I should be stopped on account of not having the proper papers. But my motto was, "Nothing venture, nothing have," and I was bent on facing the thing through. Fortunately I arrived safely at Clifton, a supply station about a dozen miles from the headquarters of the army in the field.

I sought an interview with a prominent general, but he was in rather a crusty humor and I concluded not to bother him. His adjutant was more polite and desired to employ me as a courier. I declined. I told him that I was an independent, paying my own expenses and that the only thing I wanted was an opportunity to fight.

General Beauregard was in command of the entire army, but I felt a hesitation in approaching him after the rebuff I had received. Thinking that the shortest way to get what I wanted was to obtain a regular commission, I offered an officer five hundred dollars for his. He would not sell, however, and I went over to Brigadier General Bonham, who was holding Mitchell's Ford, and introduced myself to him. General Bonham looked at me sharply and asked what company I belonged to.

"To none," I replied. "I belong wherever there is work to do."

"Well," said Bonham, "you are the right sort to have around when a fight is going

Lt. Buford fires a last shot at the enemy.

on. If you stay here a little while, I reckon you will be able to find plenty of work."

I took this as a hint to make myself at home.

At half past twelve o'clock, on the eighteenth, the enemy made a sharp attack, but did not do any great damage. Our pickets fell slowly back across the Ford. For some time a rapid but irregular firing was kept up between the contending armies. The enemy, finding us too strong, was forced to retreat. I fired a last shot at them with a dead man's musket. During the greater part of this fight, the men belonging to the two armies were often not more than a few feet from each other and it seemed more like a series of duels than anything such as I had imagined a battle would be.

This skirmish was but the prelude to Manassas, or Bull Run - the first great battle of the war - which was fought on the twenty-first of July, 1861. It served to initiate me, and to make me impatient to have an opportunity to make a display of my fighting qualities. I had been placed in command of a company, the senior officer of which had been killed, and I was afraid that if a fight was long delayed I should be superseded. Men did harder fighting at Bull Run than myself, but none went through the fight with a stouter heart.

At daybreak on the nineteenth I was ready to march. Passing through Ashby's Gap, we reached the little town of Piedmont. On the twentieth, General Johnston arrived at Manassas about noon, and was followed by two Georgia regiments and Jackson's brigade of gallant Virginians. Then came Bernard E. Bee, with the fourth Alabama regiment, the second regiment, and three companies of the eleventh regiment of Mississippians.

I followed Bee's line through a dense wood. General Bee appointed me a special messenger and sent me with an order to Colonel Wheat, of the Louisiana battalion, and to General Evans, whom I had heard much talk of. He looked very much as if the kind of liquor he was in the habit of drinking did not agree with him.

On the morning of the day of the battle, I was awake at dawn. Some of the men around me had laughed at the efforts of the dandified independent to get a chance to display his valor, but not one of them was more eager to fight than myself. If I had allowed myself to be irritated by snubs from officers, I should have gone back to Richmond in disgust before the battle came off and resumed the garb of my sex with a determination never to figure as a man again. I had no thought of turning back for any cause, no matter what might be said or thought of me.

I labored under some disadvantages in not having a regular commission and not being attached to a regular command. This exposed me to slights that would otherwise not have been put on me. On the other hand, my being an independent enabled me to choose my own position in the battle, and I probably, therefore, had a better opportunity of distinguishing myself. This I did and was highly elated at the commendations the best soldiers bestowed upon the "plucky little devil," as they called me.

The supreme moment of my life had arrived, and all the glorious aspirations of my romantic girlhood were on the point of realization. Fear was a word I did not know the meaning of upon the battlefield where the Confederate troops first gave the enemy a taste of their genuine quality and achieved their first great victory.

It soon became apparent that the position in which fortune had placed me was to be the chief point of the Federal attack and that my comrades would bear the brunt of the battle. Colonel Wheat was severely wounded, but he succeeded in checking the advance of the enemy. The Federals were in strong force, fifteen thousand immediately in front of us. The commands of Bee, Evans, and Bartow were all soon engaged in resisting the advance

The Battle of Bull Run

of superior numbers and had quite as much as they could attend to to do it. I attached myself to my favorite officer, Bee, and remained with his command during the entire day.

The Federal artillery, which sent its shells showering over us and bursting in our ranks, creating terrible slaughter, was commanded by an acquaintance of mine, Ricketts. I did the best I could to give him as good as he sent, for the sake of old times when we were friends, and when neither of us imagined that we would someday be opposite each other on the battlefield. The Confederates, although greatly outnumbered, succeeded for a long time in maintaining their ground. Our men suffered terribly, the seventh Georgia and fourth Alabama regiments especially. At length, despite all our efforts, Bee was compelled to give the order for us to fall back. The Federals thought that the victory was theirs when they saw us retreat. It was a terrible moment, and my heart fell when I heard Bee's order. I was overcome with rage and indignation, and felt all the shame and mortification of a personal defeat.

Bee rallied his men with a voice of thunder, saying, "My boys, at them again! Victory or death! See how Jackson stands there like a stone wall." This last expression seemed to please the men, for they took it up immediately; and with a cheer for "Stonewall" Jackson, they made another dash at the enemy.

At noon the battle was at its fiercest, and the scene was grand beyond description. The red dust from the parched roads arose in clouds in every drection, while the smoke from the musketry floated aloft in fantastic columns, marking the places where the battle was being fought with the most bitterness. Hard pressed by the superior Federal force, our men wavered and fell back; at one time there was every prospect of panic. We were spared this disgrace by the personal exertions of Beauregard and Johnston, who darted along the line and succeeded in rallying the men. General Johnston turned the fortunes of the day by charging on the enemy, with the colors of the fourth Alabama at his side. The personal examples of Generals Beauregard, Johnston, and other prominent officers who plunged into the melee had an immense effect in encouraging the men to resist to the last.

At two o'clock the right of Beauregard's line was ordered to advance to recover the plateau. Stonewall Jackson succeeded in piercing the enemy's center, but his troops suffered terribly in doing so. Bee, while leading his fourth Alabama regiment in a charge, fell mortally wounded. Fifty yards north, Bartow was shot. His last words were, "Boys, I am killed; but don't give up the field."

The conflict was now more bitter than ever. At this crisis, a courier came up to me with a message for General Johnston that the Federals had reached the line of the Manassas Gap Railroad and were marching on us with heavy force. Fortunately, the advancing troops were those of Kirby Smith, two thousand infantry and Beekman's artillery. The arrival of this force decided the fate of the battle, and the Federals fled, defeated, from the field.

After the battle I appealed to General Jackson for the promotion I had earned, and he gave me a recommendation to General Bragg for a recruiting commission. This I did not care about, for I thought that I did not need his permission to do recruiting. I remained for some time with the Louisiana regiment, hoping that another battle would begin. There was no prospect of a fight very soon and, becoming tired of inactivity, I determined to return to Richmond to find some work suited to my abilities.

Chapter Five

I have remarked that the men seemed to be under the idea that they were going on a pleasant holiday excursion rather than engaging in a serious business which would demand all their energies. I confess that I was not free from the feeling. The young fellows, like my Arkansas recruits, were glad of any pretext for getting away from their dismal surroundings and thought that fighting the Yankees would be good fun. The expression constantly heard, that one Southerner could whip five Yankees was not mere bounce; it represented what nearly everybody thought. Few had any doubt as to the speedy end of the conflict, or that it would end in the recognition of Southern independence.

In many respects, the victory at Bull Run was anything but a benefit to the South. The panic which overtook the Federal soldiers only inspired them with a determination to wipe out the disgrace. They hurried men to the front with such rapidity that they soon had a force in the field which compelled the Confederates to act upon the defensive. On the other hand, not only the men who fought at Bull Run, but the whole South, were elated at having won the first great battle - and were more impressed than ever with the idea that whipping the Yankees was a remarkably easy thing to do.

The result of this was that discipline was relaxed, and hundreds of good fighting men were permitted to go home. Others lounged around the camps, or went to Richmond, for the purpose of having a good time when they ought to have been following up their success by further blows at the enemy. It is easy enough now to see the mistakes that were made. I do not pretend that I was any wiser at the time, or that I had any appreciation of the magnitude of the task we had before us. Experience, in this case, was too late in giving her instructions for it to do any good.

The victory at Bull Run was most demoralizing to Richmond, the capital of the Confederacy. Crowds of soldiers thronged the streets when they ought to have been on duty in the field. Money was entirely too plentiful, and the drinking saloons, gambling houses, and worse resorts reaped a rich harvest. After a while, as month after month wore away, those who, like myself, had their hearts in the cause, began to be impatient and disgusted at the inactivity. I enjoyed the excitement of life in Richmond for a time, but was soon glad to get away.

After the battle of Bull Run I did as much tall talking as anybody and swaggered about in fine style, sporting my uniform for the admiration of the ladies. I began to pride myself as much upon being a successful lady's man as upon being a valiant soldier.

The only adventure of any consequence that I had in Richmond was a difficulty with a lieutenant who started a quarrel with me. Finding me apparently indisposed to have any words with him, he seemed to think he could insult me with impunity. I stood a good bit of insolence from him on account of his being in liquor, and endeavored to avoid him. As I was much smaller than himself, he thought that it was a good opportunity to air the spirit of blackguardism, which is the strongest characteristic in some people. At length I could not stand his insolence and slapped his face. He seemed stunned for a moment while I walked off, determined to take no further notice of him. When he recovered, he gave me a volley of abuse and threatened to shoot me. Fortunately, a friend stepped up and prevented him from making a fool of himself any further. I thought that perhaps he might

Lt. Buford slaps the insolent lieutenant.

attempt to revenge himself, but he came to the conclusion that discretion was the better part of valor and kept out of my way. I never saw his homely visage again.

Not being successful in getting the kind of appointment I desired at Richmond, I obtained a pass and transportation for the West. When I got as far as Lynchburg, however, I changed my mind, owing to meeting with some of the boys from Leesburg who persuaded me to go there with them, as there was every prospect of another fight coming off soon.

To Leesburg I went. I splurged around in fine style and one young lady, Miss E., showed a marked regard for me. Our acquaintance would have developed into a decided attachment had I not been sailing under false colors. I regretted that I permitted matters to go as far as they did when I found what an impression I was making on her susceptible heart. It was necessary for me to sustain the character I had assumed, and to make myself as agreeable as possible to the members of my own sex. Apart from this, much of the male society was so disagreeable to me that I was glad to escape from it by seeking lady friends. I am willing to admit that I ought not to have acted as I did, and if anything should induce me to assume male attire again, I should carefully avoid making love to young ladies. My error in allowing myself to indulge in flirtations with my own sex arose from thoughtlessness, and from a desire to play my part to the best advantage; I am sure my readers will forgive me, as I hope the young ladies whom I induced to indulge false expectations will, when the publication of this narrative makes known the truth about the identity of Lieutenant Harry T. Buford, C.S.A.

Chapter Six

It might be supposed that one battle should have been enough for me, and that after the carnage at Bull Run I should have been glad to have abandoned a soldier's career. Indeed, it turned out that the most efficient services I did perform on behalf of the cause were other than those of a strictly military character, although quite as important as any rendered by the bravest fighters when standing face to face with the enemy. We are all creatures of circumstance, and when I saw that my being a woman would enable me to play another role than I had first intended, I did not hesitate.

The Battle of Bull Run, however, only quickened my ardor to participate in another affair of a similar kind. The months of enforced inaction which succeeded that battle had the effect of making me long to experience again the excitement which thrilled me on the sultry July day when the army of the Confederacy won its first great victory. The second battle in which I participated - that at Ball's Bluff - was accompanied by every circumstance of horror. Although in the excitement of the moment, when every faculty of mind and body was at extreme tension, I was only inspired with an intense eagerness to do my whole duty for my cause. I did not realize the enormities of such a slaughter as was involved in the defeat of the Federals at that place, and I have never been able to think of it without a shudder, notwithstanding that I have fought on more than one bloody field since. Such scenes, however, are inseparable from warfare, and those who take up arms must steel themselves against them.

It was the tenth of October, 1861, when I left Leesburg and went to the headquarters of General Evans. I showed him my papers and asked to be employed. He sent me to Colonel Burt, of the eighth Virginia regiment, who told me that he had no vacancy in his command. I had no other resource now but to await events and feel disappointed at not being able to become attached to some command.

At Hunton's headquarters I had the pleasure of meeting Colonel Featherstone, of the seventh Mississippi regiment. This fine officer I had known when I was small, and I was amused at the idea of renewing my acquaintance with him. He had not the shadow of an idea that the dashing little lieutenant who stood before him was a woman whom he had known as a child. He took an interest in me, and asked questions which I had to draw extensively upon my imagination to answer in proper style.

He said, "Lieutenant, you can turn in here if you wish, if you have not been assigned to quarters. You are welcome to all I have and can make yourself at home."

The next morning, October twenty-second, I was up and ready for whatever might happen. A large force of the enemy, belonging to the command of Colonel Baker, had succeeded in crossing at Edwards' Ferry and had gained the Bluffs. The brigade, under the command of General Evans, consisted of four regiments. The first brunt of the fight was borne by Lieutenant Colonel Janifer, who, with five companies, was covering the approach to Leesburg. About twelve o'clock, the eighth Virginia regiment advanced to Janifer's assistance; this, I saw, was my chance if I wished to participate in the battle.

Immediately on top of the Bluff, there was a tolerably open piece of ground, cut up somewhat by ridges and hollows and surrounded by a thick growth of woods. It was impossible for us to tell what force we were contending with. The woods seemed to be alive with combatants, and it was thought that the enemy was strongly fortified. We attacked with spirit, and for a time the fight was bravely carried on by both armies. The enemy fought exceedingly well. We did not know at the time the attack was made that our foes were in such a desperate predicament.

Colonel Burt, with his eighteenth Mississippi regiment, advanced to the attack on the left of our line, while Janifer and the Virginians held the center. Burt's Mississippians were compelled to undergo a most terrific fire from the enemy, who were concealed in the hollows. They succeeded in holding them in check, although they suffered severely and Colonel Burt was numbered among the slain before the victory was won.

At three o'clock, Colonel Featherstone came up with his regiment, and advanced at a double-quick to the assistance of Burt. I thought the struggle at Bull Run a desperate one, but that battle at its fiercest did not begin to equal this. When we finally did succeed in routing the enemy, I experienced a sense of satisfaction and relief that was overwhelming. For three weary hours the fighting continued without intermission. As the chilly October day was about closing, the enemy had lost a great number of men and officers, including Colonel Baker, and were driven in confusion to the river.

Shortly after the fight commenced, I took charge of a company which had lost its officers, and I do not think that either my men or myself failed to do our full duty. In this battle, fighting as we were for the most part in the woods, there was little or no maneuvering to be done, and my main duties were to keep the men together, and to set an example.

After the battle was over, the first lieutenant of the company which I was commanding came in and relieved me, stating that he had been taken prisoner but had succeeded in making his escape in the confusion incident to the Federal defeat. I had serious doubts as to the story he told. He had a sheepish look, as if he were ashamed of himself for playing a cowardly trick, and I shall always believe that when firing commenced, he found an op-

Ball's Bluff

portunity to slink away to the rear for the purpose of getting out of the reach of danger. I have seen a good many officers like this, brave enough when strutting about in the streets of cities, showing off their uniforms to the women, or when airing their authority in camp by bullying soldiers under them, but who were the most arrant cowards under fire, and who ought to have been court-martialled and shot, instead of being permitted to disgrace their uniforms, and to demoralize their men.

The daylight was beginning to fail when the enemy broke and ran toward the river, a confused mob of fugitives instead of an organized and disciplined army. I was so wearied that I could scarcely stand. But at this moment I would rather have died than faltered. All my Southern blood was stirred in my veins. General Evans gave orders to drive our foes to the river, or to capture them, and every man seemed animated to defeat the enemy. I advanced my company saying, "They are badly whipped, I think!"

Looking under me into a little ravine, I espied a Yankee sergeant reaching for a musket, evidently with the intention of treating me to its contents. Levelling a pistol at him I cried out, "No, you don't! Drop that and come here, you scoundrel!"

He obeyed me in short order, and when he had reached me I said, "What do you mean by that? If it wasn't for having the name of murdering a prisoner, I would shoot you."

He answered sullenly, and I don't believe that he cared much, for he felt badly at having been defeated.

While talking with this prisoner, a number of other fugitives were discovered hidden in the gullies whom I immediately captured.

At the point where I stood, the Potomac River was very wide, and it presented a sight such as I prayed I'd never behold again. The enemy were driven down the Bluff; crowds of them were floundering in the water, grappling with death. This horrible spectacle made me shudder for, although they were my foes, they were still human beings, and my heart must have been hard, indeed, could it not have felt for their sufferings.

All the woman in me revolted at the fiendish delight which some of our soldiers displayed at the sight of the terrible agony endured by those who had, a short time before, been contesting the field so valiantly. I could scarcely refrain from making some effort to put a stop to the carnage, to relieve my suffering foes. For the first time since putting on my uniform I was thrown off my guard and should have done something to betray my secret had I not restrained myself. The pitiable spectacles which followed our victory at Ball's Bluff satisfied my appetite for fighting for some time. I was by no means as anxious for another battle as I had been after the victory at Bull Run.

When the enemy broke before the galling fire we poured into them, they stampeded the river, a disordered, panic-stricken crowd. Over the Bluff they went, pell-mell, leaping, rolling and tumbling, more like a herd of frightened buffalo fleeing from the savages of the plains than human beings. Hundreds were shot down while attempting to cross; others were captured before they could gain the river.

Directly, one of the prisoners I was guarding shouted, "There goes my colonel!"

I said, "I hope the poor fellow will get safely to land, for he has fought bravely, and deserves a better fate than a watery grave."

Colonel Devens was a powerful swimmer, for he was soon out of musket-shot, and managed to gain the other shore.

When the rout began, there was but one boat in the river, and this was quickly filled

After the Battle of Ball's Bluff

with a struggling mass of humanity, each man being intent only on making good his escape from the deadly fire of the Confederates. A large number of those who plunged into the river were drowned in the icy water; the shrieks of these poor fellows rang in my ears for days afterward.

I fired my revolver at another officer - a major, I believe - who was in the act of jumping into the river. I saw him spring into the air and fall; I then turned my head away, shuddering at what I had done. An officer near me exclaimed, "Lieutenant, your ball took him!" These words sent a thrill of horror through me.

The most awful episode of the day was the sinking of the boats containing the wounded and dying; from this I turned away, sick at heart, unable to endure the sight of it.

So ended the battle of Ball's Bluff. The soldiers of the Confederacy had won another great victory, although at a terrible sacrifice, for many of our bravest officers and men were slain, and a great number severely wounded. I had the satisfaction of knowing that I had fought bravely. It cost me a pang to think of the noble fellows who fell in defense of the cause they loved, and I particularly mourned the death of the gallant Colonel Burt.

When the night closed upon the battlefield and put an end to the carnage, I was used up by fatigue. Not even the terrible scenes which haunted me could prevent me from dropping into a dreamless sleep.

Chapter Seven

It fretted me to lounge about camp, or to participate in the demoralizing amusements of the city as I had been compelled to do for many weeks after the fight at Bull Run. I was disgusted, too, at the difficulties which presented themselves at every step whenever I attempted to get myself attached to a regular command, or to be assigned the kind of service for which I felt best qualified. It was a necessity for me to be doing something, and the slow progress of the military annoyed me. The reaction after the excitements of the battle of Ball's Bluff caused a depression which I felt I must shake off. The sights and sounds of the battle haunted me; the more I thought of them, the more horrible they appeared.

I determined to put into execution a project I had for some time been meditating. Before entering the career of soldier, I knew a great deal about military life, having been the wife of an officer. I nevertheless had superficial notions about the exigencies of warfare. I was soon disillusioned that actual warfare was far different from what I had supposed it would be. Neither of the battles I had thus far been engaged in impressed me. Battles, I found, were likely to be few and far between, while there were thousands of disagreeable incidents connected with military life which I had never suspected - and of which my husband's warnings had scarcely given me the slightest hint. I soon awakened to the fact that in a great war, it was not always the men who wore the uniforms and handled the muskets who performed the most efficient services. As there were other things besides fighting to do, so there must be other than soldiers to aid in advancing the cause.

It is good to do one's duty quietly amid the rush of great events, even when the path of duty lies in hidden places, and one's own satisfaction at duty nobly performed is the best recompense. To be a second Joan of Arc was mere girlish fancy which my first experience as a soldier dissipated forever. It did not take me long to discover that I needed no model—

to win success in the career I had chosen, I must be simply myself and not a copy of anybody else. The secret of success consists of watching the current of events and in taking advantage of circumstances as they arise. In a life as novel as I was now leading, I was obliged to go ahead at random and to wait and learn what there was for me to do. A woman like myself who had a talent for assuming disguises, was possessed of courage, resolution and energy backed up by a ready wit, plausible address and attractive manners, had it in her power to perform many services of the most vital importance, impossible for a man to even attempt.

The rumors that prevailed of the enormous preparations being made by the Federal government to crush the South, an insatiable desire to see and to hear for myself what was going on within the enemy's lines, all stimulated me to make an attempt, the hazardous character of which I well knew. I chafed under the ennui of the camp, and felt impelled to be doing something that, whatever its result might be, would give me the excitement I craved.

A woman labors under some disadvantages in an attempt to fight her own way in the world. I wish I had been created a man instead of a woman. But, being a woman, I was bent on making the best of it; and having for some time now figured successfully in the garments of the other sex, I resolved upon resuming those of my own for a season, for the purpose I had in mind. This purpose I felt sure I could accomplish as a woman.

Having obtained a letter of introduction to General Leonidas Polk, and my transportation papers, I turned in my camp equipage to the quartermaster and, bidding farewell to my friends, started off in search of new adventures. Stopping in Leesburg, I went, in company with a couple of other officers, to pay a visit to Mrs. Tyree, a true-hearted Virginia lady. We tried to persuade her to remove to a safer locality, representing that the Federals were likely to repeat the attack at any time, and to march on Leesburg with a large force. Our appeals were in vain. She answered every argument by saying, "This is my home, and I will perish in it, if necessary." I said adieu to her with the sincerest admiration for her inflexible courage and devotion to the South.

I stated to my acquaintances that I intended to make a journey, but did not tell anyone where I was going, or what my plans were. I felt that the success of my project depended upon my secret being kept to myself. What I dreaded more than any danger I was likely to be exposed to was the ridicule that would probably meet me in case of failure or of my sex being discovered. The way to keep a secret, as I have long since found out, is not to tell anybody.

It was necessary, however, for me to have some assistance in getting started, as it had been for me to select a confidante when I first assumed the uniform of an officer, and I would say here that, to the infinite honor of the friend whose aid I sought on that occasion, the secret was faithfully kept. As the circumstances were different, a different kind of agent was in this case selected.

Going to an old negro woman who had washed for me, I told her that I intended visiting the Yankees for the purpose of seeing them about coming and freeing the slaves, and asked her to let me have a suit of women's clothes so that I could get through the lines without being stopped. She was not long in having me attired in the best she had—a calico dress, a woolen shawl, a sunbonnet, and a pair of shoes much too large for me—and hiding away my uniform where it would be safe during my absence. The old woman put such faith in me that I felt sorry at deceiving her, but lying is as necessary as fighting in warfare.

I found an old man who had a boat and, making up a story, struck a bargain with him to take me across to the Maryland shore for twenty-five dollars. He warned me that it would be risky, for the weather was cold, the river broad and deep, and the current strong. There was considerable danger of my being fired at by the pickets on either bank. I concealed myself in his cabin until the time for the crossing arrived, neither of us deeming it prudent to start before midnight.

We launched our little craft on the black, swift-running water of the Potomac, and it was three hours before we reached the Maryland side of the river. I was numb with cold and stiff in all my limbs. Dismissing the boatman I made my way to a farm house a short distance from the landing. About four o'clock in the morning I crept into a wheat stack and slept there until daylight.

I scarcely know whether to say I enjoyed this or not. For a thinly-clad woman to find no better place for repose during a chilly night in October, after having endured the cutting blasts for three hours while crossing the Potomac in an open boat, was certainly hard lines. I had accustomed myself to rough living, but this was rougher than anything I had experienced. As there was no one but myself to applaud my heroism, this episode did not have the same attraction that some even more perilous ones had; yet I had a certain amount of pleasure in it. My enjoyment I can attribute to my insatiable love for adventure, to the same overmastering desire to do difficult, dangerous, and exciting things, and to accomplish hazardous enterprises, that had induced me to assume the dress of the other sex, and to figure as a soldier on the battlefield.

I managed to get a nap for a couple of hours, and was awakened by increasing light and by the noises of the farmyard. Adjusting my clothing as well as I could and shaking off the straw that clung to me, I approached the house. A man came out to meet me and looked at me as if he thought me a suspicious character. My appearance was such that there was certainly good cause for distrust. The old woman's calico dress, woolen shawl, sunbonnet, and shoes did not come near fitting me, while my slumbers in the wheat-stack had not tended to make me an attractive object. I was a perfect fright, and was amused rather than displeased with the discourteous reception I met with.

Plucking up courage, I advanced and told him that I had been driven out of Virginia, and was trying to get back to my people in Tennessee. I asked him if I could not go into the house and warm myself and get some breakfast, as I was both cold and hungry. I suppose I looked so pitiful that he felt compelled to grant my request. He invited me into the dining room and called his wife.

The woman invited me to a nice warm breakfast and, taking pity on my mean attire, insisted on dressing me in some of her own clothing. I was soon in a presentable condition and able to reach my destination. I bade them good-bye and started for Washington, where I hoped to make what soldiers call a reconnaissance in force.

Chapter Eight

Having penetrated the lines of the enemy, there was, I knew, little to fear. I passed for exactly what I was, and felt secure moving about as I chose, having a plausible story to tell anybody who might question me. I concluded that, as it was most likely I would meet

Crossing the Potomac

Sleeping in the wheat stack

people who knew me as a woman, it would be safer to figure as myself and as nobody else.

Between my starting point on the Maryland side of the river and Washington, I saw a good many soldiers - from which I judged that the approaches to the Federal capital were strongly guarded. This was important information I succeeded in obtaining. There were matters better worth knowing than this that I hoped to discover, and to discover them it was necessary for me to go to Washington to obtain facilities for conversing with people who knew what I wanted to know.

On arriving, I went to Brown's Hotel, and having learned that an officer of the regular Federal army, with whom I was well acquainted and who had been a warm, personal friend of my late husband, was in the city, I sent him a note, asking him to call on me. Greeting me with cordiality, he expressed a desire to aid me in any manner that lay in his power. I began to question him about the progress of the war. He spoke without any reserve concerning a number of matters about which he would certainly have kept silent had he suspected that I had just come from the other side of the Potomac, and that my object was to pick up information useful to the Confederacy.

He lamented the defeat which the Federals had met with at Ball's Bluff, and from what he said I judged that the affair was the great sensation of the hour. My friend was blue when discussing the subject, and expressed himself in very energetic terms with regard to the rebels, little thinking he was conversing with one who had played a most active part in the very thickest of battle. He went on to say that the defeat at Ball's Bluff would be compensated for shortly, and that in Kentucky the Federals were making great preparations for an active campaign. I succeeded in obtaining a few points from him, but he was apparently not informed with the particulars. It is probable too, that he knew a good deal that he did not choose to tell even me, unsuspicious as he was about my real character.

The information of most vital moment that I succeeded in obtaining from him, however, was that active preparations were being made to secure possession of the upper Mississippi, and that a large fleet was being fitted out for the purpose of blockading the mouth of the river. I surmised that an attack on New Orleans was in contemplation, and resolved to find out the actual intentions of the Federal government. By the time I left Washington, I was convinced that a grand blow was shortly to be struck, either at Mobile or New Orleans, but most likely in the latter city. I pumped, in a quiet way, everybody I met who was at all likely to know anything. I was afraid to push my inquiries too far, though, as I did not care to be suspected as a spy and put under surveillance. I learned that the government was annoyed by the presence of numbers of Confederate spies in Washington, and was disposed to deal vigorously with them if they were caught. This was simply a reconnoitering expedition, undertaken entirely on my own account, without authority from anybody.

My friend took his departure, promising to call the next day to take me to the different places of interest. This was exactly what I wanted, for I was desirous of being informed, as soon as possible, exactly where the public offices were situated. He made his appearance promptly the next morning and took me to see the Patent Office, the Treasury Department, and the War Department. I led him up to making a proposal that he should introduce me to the Secretary of War. In a demure way, I expressed myself as delighted at the honor of being able to meet so great a man and, so, in a few moments more, I was bowing, in my politest manner, to Secretary Cameron.

My conversation with him scarcely amounted to more than an exchange of the most ordinary civilities. He was abundantly courteous in his manners, but there was a crafty look in his eyes that I thought indicated a treacherous disposition. In spite of his evident knowingness, I left him feeling that I could prove myself a match for him in case our wits were ever brought into conflict.

I was much better pleased with General Wessells, the Commissary General of Prisoners, to whom I was also introduced. I decided that I was likely to make more out of him that I was out of the secretary. I said, in a careless sort of way, that I had a brother who was a prisoner, and whom I would like to see, notwithstanding that he was on the wrong side. General Wessells said that I could see him if I wished. I thanked him.

From the War Department we went to the White House, where my friend said he would introduce me to the President. I had some dread of this interview, although I experienced a great curiosity to see Mr. Lincoln. I had heard a great deal about him, of course, and not much of that was favorable, either in regards to his character or his personal appearance, I considered him a very homely man, but he had a pleasant, kindly face and a pleasantly familiar manner. My interview, brief as it was, induced me to believe, not only that he was not a bad man, but that he was an honest and well-meaning one. I left the White House, if not with a genuine liking for him, at least with many of my prejudices dispelled.

My change of sentiment with regard to Mr. Lincoln did not influence me with regard to my opinions concerning the contest between the North and the South. I was simply trying to do my duty, just as I suppose he was trying to do his.

After leaving the White House, we visited the Capitol and listened to the debates in Congress for awhile. I had more pleasure in looking about the noble building, though, than in hearing them talk.

Our next visit was to the Post Office. Here I succeeded in finding out a number of things I wanted to know and obtained some really important information, simply by listening to the conversation I heard going on around me. I was really annoyed at some of what I heard between government officials while at the Post Office. I wondered how the Federal authorities ever expected to prevent the Confederates from finding out their plans if this kind of thing was going on all the time.

My tour convinced me that Washington would be a first-rate place to operate in if I could obtain an attachment to the detective corps. I had the abilites to put the Confederate authorities in possession of information of the first value. Having fulfilled my errand, I left Washington as suddenly as I entered it. I had little trouble getting back to Leesburg, and put in an appearance at the house of the old woman who had my uniform hidden away for me within thirteen days from the time I left it.

Once more in the garb of a Confederate officer, I returned the old woman her calico dress, shawl, sunbonnet and shoes. The next day I was en route for Columbus, Tennessee, where I expected to find General Polk. Notwithstanding that the Confederates had won the first great victory, it became apparent at an early day that a single battle was not going to finish the war. If the South was to achieve its independence, it must go through a long and bloody conflict.

The chill winds of winter were beginning to make their severity felt by the poor soldiers. I was prepared for a long and desperate war.

Chapter Nine

A few days of hard travel and I was back at Memphis, having made the circuit of the entire Confederacy east of the Mississippi. The friend of whom I have spoken I still found

Loreta meets President Abraham Lincoln.

in Memphis, now captain in the Confederate service. I related my adventures, and he made no attempt to dissuade me from my purpose. I took the first boat for Columbus, where I expected to find General Polk. He received me cordially, although he dismissed me with the indefinite observation that he would see what he could do. I was not pleased when I found that I was to run on the cars as military conductor, and I tendered my resignation shortly, as I preferred service in the field to duty like this.

I received an urgent letter from my friend, Captain Shankey, asking me to return to Virginia and enter the secret service. It was my intention to go back, and it would, perhaps, have been better for me if I had. If everything happened to us just as we desired, adventure would lose much of its zest. My campaign in the West, before I trod Virginia ground again, was adventuresome enough. I thought there would be a chance for me in Kentucky to demonstrate my value either as a soldier or a spy. I began to look about for a good place to commence operations again. I took part in the fight at Woodsonville. Colonel Terry, whom I greatly admired, was among the slain. I decided to shift my quarters to where there was a better prospect of hard fighting. In blissful ignorance of the agonizing scenes which I would soon be called upon to witness, I started for Fort Donelson.

I entered this conflict with different emotions from those which animated me when about to take part in the battle of Bull Run. Then I was inspired by all the enthusiasm of ignorance. I could not get rid of the idea that the rout of the enemy would mean their annihilation. I did not think. I only felt, just like thousands of others.

The Federals made their appearance on the afternoon of Wednesday the twelfth, and they could be seen at various points through the woods making preparations for commencing their attack. The weather suddenly became intensely cold. On Thursday night a tremendous storm of snow and sleet came on. A young officer had made an arrangement for me to go on picket duty for him in the trenches. I confess that the sleet stung my face and the biting winds cut me to the bones; I wished myself well out of it.

The agonized cries of the wounded, and their piteous calls for water, affected me more than my own discomfort. I could face the cannon better than I could this bitter weather, and I could suffer myself better than I could bear to hear the cries and groans of these wounded men, lying out on the frozen ground, exposed to the beatings of this pitiless storm. Several times I felt as if I could stand it no longer, and was tempted to give the whole thing up and lie down upon the ground and die. I understood from this brief experience what must have been the sufferings of the army of Napoleon, on the retreat from Moscow; the story which had seemed a romance now presented to my mind a terrible reality.

On Friday the forces on the land side did not attempt any serious demonstrations. It was now the turn of the gunboats to drive us out of the fort. The navy did not have any better success than the army. The boats commenced to shell our works, but they inflicted on us no particular damage, while our fire told on them with terrible effect. The gunboats continued for about an hour and a half, at the end of which time we had the satisfaction of seeing them drift down the river, badly cut up. The end of the second day's battle was in favor of the Confederates. In the meantime, the besieging army was receiving large reinforcements, and preparing to renew the attack on the land side with increased vigor.

The Confederate commanders resolved not to wait to be attacked, but to sally from the fort and strike the enemy with a deadly blow. The contest was conducted with terrible vigor on both sides for some hours. Our men succeeded in driving back the Federals, but

On Picket Duty at Fort Donelson

with great loss. At length, the Federals rallied and stormed the entrenchments with a much larger force than before. After a severe struggle the Confederates were driven back into the fort, leaving hundreds of the dead and wounded lying on the frozen ground. By this time our ranks had been so thinned out that everyone felt it would be madness to continue the contest longer against the greatly superior force of the enemy. The Federals were masters of the field and all we cared to do was to get as many of our men as possible away before the surrender took place.

This was undoubtedly one of the most terrible battles of the whole war. Towards the last, the contest between besiegers and besieged was hand to hand, both sides contending for mastery with a ferocity I cannot describe. Again and again were the Federals repulsed from the works; they were so much cut up that it seemed impossible for them to rally again. Reinforcements of fresh troops, however, came continually to the relief of the defeated assailants, while each hour thinned out the garrison terribly.

In every direction the ground was trampled by thousands of feet; cut up by the artillery carriages; and strewn with dead horses, men, and all kinds of munitions of war. In many of the trenches, especially where the fiercest fighting had taken place, the bodies were heaped together, six or seven feet high. The faces of the corpses, distorted with the agonies of their death struggles, were hideous to look at. Those who fell and died where they were shot were comparatively fortunate, for their sufferings were soon ended. It was sickening to think of the many poor fellows who, after fighting bravely and falling helpless from their wounds, had their lives crushed out, and their forms mangled beyond recognition, by the furiously driven artillery.

Some of the men, with their limbs fearfully mangled, pleaded most piteously not to have them amputated, many of them stating that they preferred death to this new torture. Others could do no more than groan, or utter such cries as, "God help me;" while not a few besought the surgeons to kill them. It was no wonder Dr. Moore said that it was no place for women and that it was as much as the strong nerves of a man could do to bear up under such an accumulation of horrors.

Immediately after the defeat at Fort Donelson, I was greatly depressed in spirit; it was long before I could shake off the disposition to shudder and the feeling of intense melancholy. I almost resolved to give up the whole business. In course of time, however, with restored health - I was quite sick from the exposures, fatigues, and horrors of the battle - my spirits regained their elasticity. It was never my disposition to brood over misfortunes, and after a little rest I was ready to resume my life as a soldier of fortune.

Chapter Ten

From Fort Donelson I went, with what speed I could, to Nashville, and took rooms at the St. Cloud Hotel. I needed an opportunity to thoroughly rest. It was an immense relief to have shelter over my head, a comfortable bed, and wholesome food. Such was the agitation of my mind on account of the terrible scenes through which I had passed, though, that I could not keep quiet. I recovered a little from my fatigue, then was eager to be in motion again. I was as anxious as ever to do a soldier's full duty. If ever my services were needed, they were needed now. I went to the headquarters of General Johnston and was put in the detective corps. I had no reason to complain of lack of activity.

The Confederates are driven back to Fort Donelson.

While participating in a skirmish with the enemy, who were harassing us whenever an opportunity arose, I was wounded in the foot. This lamed me, and compelled me to have the hurt dressed by the surgeon, at which I was not a little alarmed, for I knew that I was now in imminent danger of having my sex discovered. Dreading the prospect of being under the care of a surgeon, I resolved that the only course for me was to abandon the army before I got into trouble. I quietly slipped away to Grand Junction, where I remained for three days, and then repaired to Jackson, Mississippi. I hastened without further delay to New Orleans, and took up my quarters at the Brooks House.

I had managed to sustain myself in the army as an independent without difficulty, and was on the best possible terms with everybody. In New Orleans I found the spirit of suspicion rampant. The Federals were known to be mustering an enormous fleet at the mouth of the river, and a large army on the Sound. My surmises of months before, based upon what I had heard in Washington, were apparently about to be realized. The fear of Federal spies was in the hearts of many.

During the eight or nine months I had been wearing male attire, I had seen a great deal of very hard service. My clothing was well-worn, and my apparatus for disguising my form was badly out of order. The result was that I scarcely presented as creditable a manly appearance as I did upon the occasion of my last visit to New Orleans. In addition to this, I was in very low spirits, if not absolutely sick, when I reached the town, and was not in a mood to play my part in the best manner.

I had not been in the city very long before it was noted by prying people that there was some mystery about me. I was arrested on the charge of being a spy, and taken before the provost marshal. I feared my great secret was now on the point of being discovered. I was enraged at the idea of being charged with acting as a spy and of having my patriotism doubted after all I had done to promote the cause of Southern independence. I determined that the best - if not the only - plan was to present a bold front and to challenge my accusers to prove anything against me.

I entered a vigorous protest to the officer who made the arrest, and I could see he had no definite charge against me. My protest, however, was to no avail, for the officer insisted upon my accompanyng him to the office of the provost marshal. He questioned me closely, and I soon saw that he was beginning to doubt whether he was doing the correct thing in making the arrest. To the office of the provost marshal we went. That official decided, with gratifying promptness, that there was no justification for holding me, and ordered my discharge from custody.

This incident gave me a great deal of uneasiness. I was not much surprised, although greatly disgusted, when the next evening I was again arrested, this time on suspicion of being a woman. Being taken before Mayor Monroe, I was interrogated in a style that I did not admire. He chose to assume that I was a woman, and ordered me to change my apparel. Turning to him, I said with severity, "Sir, prove that I am a woman, and it will be quite time, when you do that, for you to give me an order to change my dress."

They were doubtful how to proceed, being uncertain whether or not they had made a mistake. My hopes of a prompt discharge were doomed, for the mayor, after a brief consultation, decided to remand me to the calaboose until it should be settled to his satisfaction who I was and whether I was a man or a woman.

Lt. Buford is wounded in the foot.

There I was visited by Dr. Root of the Charity Hospital. Before he got through questioning me I was convinced that his mind was made up. I felt sure that the easiest method was to confess frankly to the mayor that I was a woman. I wrote a note to his honor, requesting a private interview. Without any more equivocation I told him who I was and gave him what I hoped would be satisfactory reasons for assuming the garb I wore. Mr. Monroe, having gotten me in his clutches, was not disposed to let me go easily. He fined me ten dollars, and sentenced me to ten days' imprisonment. I thought this was pretty rough treatment, considering all I had done to serve the Confederacy. I resolved not to give the whole thing up. I concluded that the best plan was to suffer in silence and to allow the mayor to have what satisfaction he could get out of my ten dollars and ten days.

As soon as possible after obtaining my release, I proceeded to the recruiting office at the corner of Jefferson and Chatham Streets, and enlisted in Captain B. Moses' company, of the twenty-first Louisiana regiment. The next day, we started for Fort Pillow to join the balance of the regiment. In this manner I contrived to get clear of New Orleans, but I had no fancy for going on duty as a private soldier. I went to General Villipigue and, showing my commission, told a plausible story to account for my enlistment, and asked him to give me employment as an officer. He was not able to do anything for me. I applied for a transfer to the army of East Tennessee and was very cheerfully granted it.

I was not in a very happy frame of mind, and my physical condition was scarcely better than my mental. I had not recovered from the suffering caused by the contest at Fort Donelson. After ten days' sojourn in prison, however, it was a great relief to feel that I had my destiny in my own hands once more. I dismissed the past and made a fresh start with all the energy I could command.

Chapter Eleven

Fort Donelson was to be avenged. The Federals were now concentrating in force at Pittsburg Landing, on the Tennessee River, their immediate object of attack evidently being Corinth. General Albert Sydney Johnston, who was in command of the entire Confederate army, resolved upon striking a vigorous blow at once. We all knew that a surprise was to be attempted, and all felt confident of its success—although some hard fighting was expected before the rout of the Federals could be achieved. My thoughts turned to Bull Run and Ball's Bluff, where Southern valor had so signally displayed itself, and where I had assisted in sending a routed and panic-stricken mob from the field. Notwithstanding the fact that I was a woman, I was as good a soldier as any man around me, and as willing as any to fight valiantly and to the bitter end.

Mounting my horse, I set off at a smart pace for General Hardee's headquarters. I found the general near Shiloh Church, and rode up and saluted him just as he was mounting his horse. Showing him my pass, I said that I wanted to have a hand in the affair. Hardee looked at my pass and replied, "All right; fall in, and we'll see what can be done for you."

I fell in with his men, and we advanced upon the enemy's camp. Many of the enemy were only half dressed and were obliged to snatch up the first weapons that came to hand as the Confederates rushed out of the woods upon them. We took possession of their camp, with all its equipage, and I thought that this was an excellent beginning of the day's work. I

Lt. Buford enlists in the 21st Louisiana Regiment.

The attack on the Union camp at Shiloh

had the pleasure of eating a capital hot breakfast which had been prepared for some Federal officer. I had scarcely finished eating when I espied the Arkansas boys whom I had enlisted at Hulburt Station nearly a year before. I was seized with a desire to go into the fight with them. I told Captain De Caulp that I was anxious to have a hand in the fight, especially to go into the thing with this company. I spoke in a sufficiently loud tone for the other officers and men to understand that I belonged to the special corps, and was doing a share of the fighting just for the love of the thing. Captain De Caulp told me to remain with him, and to wait and see what would happen to my advantage. In the meantime, I could act as a sort of aide to him. I considered it a rare piece of good fortune that I was able to take part in what all hoped and expected would be a decisive battle with my own company - as fine a body of men as were in the field - and there were special reasons for jubilation at the idea of being permitted to fight by the side of Captain De Caulp.

The secret might as well be told now, I suppose. Please know that Captain De Caulp and I were under an engagement of marriage, having been in correspondence with each other since my departure from Pensacola. I had his letters in my breast pocket, and his photograph in the lining of my coat. I doubt not that he had about him memorials of myself, if he cared as much for me as I was led to believe by the fervency of his epistles. I was the especial object of his thoughts when we dashed at the enemy. He little suspected, however, that the woman to whom his heart and hand were pledged was by his side as he led his men into that bloody fray, for he had an acquaintance with me both as a woman and as a man, but did not know that the two were the same.

It may be thought I should have had some tremors when beholding my lover advancing into the thick of the fight. The idea of fear never occurred to me at the time. We cannot think of everything at once, and I was intent on defeating the enemy. As for him, I desired for his sake even more than on my own account that the occasion should be a glorious one.

We had not been long engaged before the second lieutenant of the company fell. I immediately stepped into his place and assumed the command of his men. Our assaults upon the enemy were made with irresistible fury. It was grander fighting than I had ever witnessed before. The bullets whistled through the air thick and fast, cutting the trees, making the branches snap and fly, splintering the fence rails, striking the wagons, or sending some poor soldier suddenly to the earth. A corporal who was by my side was shot through the heart by a Minie ball. He fell heavily against me and all of my clothing was reddened by his blood. His only words were, "Damn the Yankees! They have killed me!" He was a very handsome young man, only about twenty-two years of age.

During the afternoon I succeeded in gaining a good deal of information from a sergeant belonging to the twenty-seventh Illinois regiment. I did this by inducing him to believe that I was only in the Confederate army under compulsion and that I intended to desert at the first opportunity. From this prisoner I learned how desperate were the straits of the enemy, and how anxiously they were awaiting reinforcements. I was consequently in despair, for I saw our brillliant victory already slipping from us, when General Beauregard issued the order from headquarters at the Shiloh church for us to halt our advance.

My station was with the advanced picket line. I gave the captain to understand that I intended, under the cover of darkness, to creep as close as I could to the Federal lines with a view of trying to find out something concerning their movements. He hesitated, but gave a tacit consent. I refrained from telling my full design to my immediate companion of the picket station, and promised to give him a drink of good whiskey when I got back if he would mind his own business and not attempt to interfere.

I stole away and approached the Landing. The Federals were crowding about it in utter disorder, without any means of crossing the river. The capture of the entire army ought to have been an easy matter. One more grand charge along the entire line, in the same brilliant fashion that we had opened the battle, and every officer and man on this side of the river would either have been slain or taken prisoner.

At this moment, I felt that if I could only command our army for two good hours I would be willing to die the moment the victory was won. Beauregard could not have understood the situation or he would have pursued his advantage. Yet I could not understand how he could help knowing, not only that the Federals were in desperate straits, but that fresh troops were hurrying to their assistance.

While I was watching, a steamboat with reinforcements arrived at the Landing. Another detachment came before I withdrew, overwhelmed with grief and disgust. The two gunboats moved up to the mouth of Lick Creek, and about dark commenced throwing shells into our lines. Sometimes they burst in the air, scattering in every direction. More often they would burst just as they struck, and the pieces inflicted ugly wounds if they happened to hit anybody. Occasionally they would bury themselves in the ground and then explode, tearing holes large enough to bury a cart and horse. During the whole of the night *Tyler* and *Lexington* threw their shells steadily, and at frequent intervals, in the direction of our army.

While I was surveying from my post in the bushes, a small boat passed up the river. As it drew near I recognized General Grant. I had seen pictures of him, so I had no trouble in knowing him in spite of the darkness. My heart began to beat violently when I saw Grant, and my hand instinctively grasped my revolver. He was completely at my mercy, within easy pistol shot. My first impulse was to kill him and run the risk of all possible consequences. Had I been firmer-nerved, the great Federal general and the future president of the United States would have finished his career.

It was too much like murder, however, and I could not bring myself to do the deed, although it would have been as justifiable as any killing that takes place in warfare. I permitted Grant to escape. Had Grant fallen before my pistol, the great battle of Shiloh might have had a far different termination. To have shot him would almost certainly have insured my own destruction, for large numbers of Federals were so near me that I could plainly hear them talking, and escape would have been out of the question.

Captain De Caulp was seriously perplexed at my report, but said that attempting to instruct the general was risky. It was as much as I could do to refrain from attempting to let Beauregard know how matters were, and of running the risks of his displeasure. I finally came to the conclusion that the responsibilities were his and not mine. I had no fancy for being put under arrest and ruining my future prospects by going through my New Orleans experiences again. I knew that there would be some hot work in the morning, and felt the necessity of getting what rest I could. I threw myself on the ground and tried to sleep.

At daylight, the gunboats began to fire more rapidly than they had during the night, and we lost the advantage we might have gained by assuming the offensive. It was easy to see that victory was no longer with the Confederates and that the grievous mistake of the night before would have the terrible consequences I feared. The Federals steadily ad-

General Grant "under the gun" of Lt. Buford; Shiloh, April 6, 1862.

vanced, and we were compelled to retire before them, our exhausted men fighting desperately as they went.

About this time, a heavy cannonading commenced. On our side, Terril's battery did excellent service, and succeeded in holding the enemy at bay, giving the infantry a breathing spell that they sorely needed. For more than two hours the Confederates kept up their work in such gallant style that the enemy wavered again, and one grand charge might have routed them. Before such a charge could be made, however, heavy reinforcements arrived, under the command of General Buell, and drove us back half a mile, breaking our lines and throwing us into inextricable confusion.

When I saw clearly that the day was lost to the Confederates, I determined to leave the field and half resolved that I would give the whole thing up and never strike another blow for the Confederacy. I was so utterly worn out and wretched that I did not care what became of me. I was almost as willing to be taken prisoner as to return to Corinth to exert myself in the apparently hopeless cause of Southern independence.

Chapter Twelve

Rested by a brief slumber on the damp ground, and with thoughts of the most gloomy description filling my mind, I mounted my horse at daybreak and started to ride back to Corinth. About five miles from that city, my horse broke from me and stampeded out of sight. There was nothing to do but to bear up as bravely as possible. Plunging through the mud, I tried to make my way back to Corinth. The first camp I made was that of the eleventh Louisiana regiment, in which I had a number of friends. Obtaining a horse from the quartermaster, I started back to the battlefield.

The road was lined with stragglers, many of them suffering from severe wounds. The ground was thickly strewn with dead men and horses. I could face the deadliest fire without flinching, but I could not bear to look at these. I rode back to camp and said goodbye to my Louisiana friends, leaving them under the impression that I intended to take the train. This I probably would have done had I not fallen in with the cavalry who were starting out on scouting duty. I concluded to try a little cavalry service.

It was about dark when we set out, and we spent the night hovering about in the neighborhood of the enemy. The next day we had a little brush with a party of Federals and, after the exchange of a few shots, were compelled to retreat. After this, we came across some dead men belonging to the tenth Tennessee regiment. Carefully removing the bodies to a field nearby, we put them in a potato bin and, with a hoe, covered them, as well as we were able, with earth. The enemy was occasionally firing shells in different directions, apparently feeling for us. Sooon a shrapnel burst in our midst, killing a young fellow instantly and wounding me severely in the arm and shoulder.

I was thrown to the ground, and stunned with the suddenness of the thing. I found that I was unable to move my right arm; soon the wound began to pain me terribly. A soldier lifted me on my horse and started back to camp with me. If my horse jolted or stumbled a little, I experienced the most excruciating agony. All my manliness oozed out long before I reached camp, and my woman's nature asserted itself with irresistible force. I longed to be where there would be no necessity for continuing my disguise and I could obtain shelter, rest, and attention as a woman.

Lt. Buford is wounded by an exploding shell.

By the time we reached camp, my hand and arm were so swollen that my conductor found it necessary to rip the sleeve of my coat in order to get at the wound to bathe it in cold water. The application of the water was a slight relief, but the hurt was too serious a one for such treatment to be of service. An ambulance was procured, and I was taken to the railroad and put on the train bound South. The cars stopped at Corinth for two hours. I sent for a young surgeon I knew intimately, and asked him to do something to relieve my suffering.

He examined my arm and, as I perceived by the puzzled expression that passed over his face, he was beginning to suspect something. Guessing that further concealment would be useless, I told him who I really was. I never saw a more astonished man in my life. The idea of a woman engaging in such an adventure, and receiving such an ugly hurt, appeared to shock him. He declared that he would not take responsibility, but he would send for Dr. S. This frightened me, for I had witnessed some of that surgeon's method of dealing with wounded soldiers, and I insisted that he was too barbarous. Finally he consentd to make a careful examination.

My shoulder was found to be out of place, my arm cut, and my little finger lacerated—a disagreeable but not very dangerous wound. The surgeon applied a dressing and put my arm in a sling, after which I felt more comfortable. He then endeavored to induce me to stop at Corinth until I was better. Now that my sex was discovered, however, I was more anxious than ever to get away. I insisted on pushing on to Grenada. He went and procured transportation papers for me.

It was an immense relief when we reached Grand Junction. I found, however, that it was an impossibility to get any accommodation. I determined to push on to Grenada. I greatly benefitted from the two days of rest I took there. Not only the natural restlessness of my disposition - which my wound aggravated - but a desire to get away from the army of Tennessee before the fact that Harry T. Buford was a woman became known, induced me to move on with speed. I started for New Orleans before I was fit to travel. When I reached Jackson, I found myself too ill to proceed. I scarcely know what I should have done had not a widow and her daughter waited on me until I was able to be on the road again.

I made another start for New Orleans. Once there, though, I was not long in concluding that it would be a good place to go away from as early as possible, for I had no notion of witnessing another triumph of the enemy. I was, however, far from being strong enough to go on active duty. When the news came that the Federal fleet had passed Forts Jackson and St. Philip, I first thought of leaving quickly. A little reflection induced me to change my mind. I saw clearly that if the Federals took possession of the city I would, as a woman, have a grand field of operation. I resolved to remain and see the thing out, and the uniform of Lieutenant Harry T. Buford was carefully put away for future use. The wearer assumed the garments of a non-combatant female for the purpose of witnessing the entry of the victors into the captured city.

Chapter Thirteen

Late on the morning of the twenty-fith of April, 1862, the Federal fleet could be seen coming up the river. It must have dampened the enthusiasm of the Yankee sailors somewhat to find steamboats, cotton, and all kinds of combustible property blazing for miles along the levee. It made me shudder to see millions of dollars worth of property being destroyed. General Lovell was probably justified in giving the order he did, thereby diminishing the value of the prize which the Federals had won.

I set to work to gain the confidence of the Federal officers. Some of them I found to be gentlemanly, gratified to hear anyone—especially any woman—express Union sentiments. I took occasion to denounce the cause I loved, and soon became known as one of the few staunch advocates of the Federal government in New Orleans. My Southern friends were alienated from me, much to my sorrow, but this could not be helped. My secret, so long as I was the sole possessor of it, was safe. It was better for me to risk the temporary loss of my friends than to risk anything by an incautious word.

I had a stroke of good luck in the very beginning. An English lady, with whom I had become acquainted, was anxious to get away as soon as possible, the capture of the city by the Federals not having the most soothing effect on her nerves. I expressed a desire to purchase her passport and other foreign papers. Armed with such documents, I would be able to make a fair start against the Federals. The lady consented to part with the papers for a fair price.

Armed with my British papers, I went to the office of the provost marshal for the purpose of striking up an acquaintance. I told him that I was a Northern woman, and that my father was a New Yorker, but that I had been unable to communicate with my friends in the North and in England, or to get away. I then told him chiefly about my poverty, the wrongs I had suffered from the rebels, and the difficulty of making ends meet. I informed him that I had come from England to New Orleans with my late husband some years before the war, and that I proposed to return there as soon as I received a sufficient remittance The provost marshal expressed a willlingness to aid me in any way that lay in his power; I bowed myself out of his presence.

From Colonel Butler I obtained permits to go to Mandeville, on the other side of Lake Pontchartrain, and even to visit Mobile without being searched. I undertook to go to Robertson's Plantation for the purpose of sending some despatches to the Confederate forces stationed at Franklin. It was necessary for me to make the trip after nightfall, and to walk the entire distance of seventeen miles.

The only sounds to be heard were the barking of the alligators or the splashing of one of these monsters as he plunged into the stream at my approach. I pushed on resolutely despite the swarms of mosquitoes. Whenever I sat down to rest, these venomous insects attacked me with the greatest fury, and my face and hands were terribly bitten. Just about daybreak I reached my destination. I was foot-sore and completely tired out, but satisfied with having accomplished my errand without having been interrupted.

I found some Confederate soldiers preparing to cross the lake and going to one of them, who seemed to be in command of the party, I told him a number of things which I had thought it prudent not to commit to writing and asked him to pass the word along. Then, waiting until the boat was ready to set sail, I gave him an enclosure containing my despatches, asking him to deliver it at headquarters. Going to a house nearby, I asked for something to eat and an opportunity to rest myself. A change of garments and a substantial breakfast refreshed me immensely. I slept a good part of the day. At about eleven at night they provided me with a horse and escorted me to as near the outposts as I deemed it safe for them to go. I made my way into the city on foot, being as successful as on the night previous in eluding the pickets. On reaching my apartment, I locked myself in and went to

Loreta delivers despatches to the Confederate forces at Franklin.

bed to take a good rest.

Unluckily for me, the very thing upon which I had not calculated, and which I had no power to prevent, occurred. The officer to whom I had entrusted my despatch was captured, and the document was found upon his person. Through some means the provost marshal was informed that I was the writer, although the name signed to it was not the one he knew me by. I was placed under arrest and taken before Butler himself.

He proceeded on the theory that I was guilty of the charge made against me. I kept cool and refused to look at the matter from his point of view. As none of the witnesses who appeared were able to swear to my identity as the woman who had acted as the bearer of the despatch, I began to think that I was going to get clear without trouble.

Butler settled his podgy figure back in his chair and said, with a harsh grating voice, "Well, madam, I have been wanting you for some time, and I propose to send you to Ship Island." I felt that the real ordeal was but just commencing.

I replied, "I guess not. The law does not permit you to sentence anyone on mere hearsay, and no evidence has been produced against me."

"Are you not guilty?" asked Butler, blinking his eyes and trying to look as savage as possible.

"That is for you to prove, if you intend to punish me," I replied. "You have not succeeded in proving it yet."

"Come, come, madam," Butler struck in sharply. "I know you and your tricks."

I retorted, "You have no proof against me, and I have nothing to confess. I don't mean to confess what I didn't do."

He roared out, "Madam, if you won't confess without compulsion, I'll see whether I can't compel you. I'm going to make an example of you for the benefit of the other female spies who are hanging about this city."

I replied, as coolly as possible, "You may get in trouble, sir, if you attempt to punish an innocent woman on a scandalous charge like this."

This appeared to infuriate Butler more than ever, and he gave an order that I should be locked up in a cell in the Custom House until my case was investigated.

I turned to him with all the dignity I could command and said, "One word, sir. I am a British subject, and I claim the protection of the British flag."

Turning to the officer he said, "Take that woman to the Custom House."

The officer in charge was a gentleman in every respect, and while escorting me to the Custom House, he apologized for being compelled to perform so unpleasant a duty. Before he left, I asked if I could not have writing materials. He said that he had no authority to grant such a request. A friend of mine, hearing that I was imprisoned, came to see me and, upon my expressing a great desire to have some pens, ink, and paper, he procured them. I immediately wrote a note to Mr. Coppell, the British consul, in which I explained my situation and asked his assistance.

Mr. Coppell called upon me at once and promised to do what he could for me. He asked for my proof of British citizenship. I gave him my trunk key and the number of my room, with a description of the papers I had purchased in view of just such an emergency. He went to Butler's headquarters to demand my liberation.

Having obtained my freedom, I prepared to forsake New Orleans, and applied for a pass. This was refused me, and I saw it would be necessary for me to run the blockade. This, I was well aware, would be a particularly risky thing to attempt, but there was no alternative, except to remain in the city, in constant danger of being found out.

Loreta is confronted by General Ben "The Beast" Butler.

I had made a number of trips in different directions, sometimes with passes and sometimes without, and consequently knew exactly how to proceed. The Federal patrols were becoming more vigilant, as resolute efforts were being made to break up the Confederate spy system. I prepared to pay a good sum to anyone who would be willing to perform the services I needed. I knew that if I could make the other side of Lake Pontchartrain I would be safe. I laid my plans with a view of striking a point near the railroad, so that I could reach Jackson with the least inconvenience.

Going down to the lake, I found a fisherman and asked, "Do any rebels ever cross the lake without papers?"

"Are you a reb?" He looked at me sharply.

"They say I am," I answered.

"I might take you over if you will pay enough."

Without argument we struck a bargain.

Going home, I put on two complete suits of clothing, as it would not have answered for me to have carried any baggage, and secreted about my person all the Confederate money I had - about nine thousand dollars - and my jewelry. At the appointed time, I saw my boatman waiting. Fearful, however, of being apprehended just as I was about to start, I did not show myself at first, but crept cautiously through the bushes until I could see whether anyone was observing my movements. Finding the coast apparently clear, I made a signal to the man. He approached and took me into the boat.

In a moment more the sail was hoisted and we were speeding over the lake before a good breeze, which promised to enable me once more to give the Confederacy the benefit of my services. I had a six-shooter and had taken pains to see that it was loaded and in condition for instant use. On taking my seat in the boat, I placed my hand on this weapon; I was resolved to put it to the head of the man if he showed the slightest desire to betray me. The man, however, was faithful enough and, with the prospect of a liberal reward, was only eager to reach the other side. On landing I paid the boatman and started off for the nearest railroad station for the purpose of going to Jackson. Thus ended my career in New Orleans as a Confederate spy.

Chapter Fourteen

I was now more intent than ever upon being employed on detective and scouting duty, for which my recent residence in New Orleans had been an excellent schooling. I judged that matters ought soon to be approaching a crisis somewhere, and I resolved that if a grand movement of any kind was coming off, I must have a hand in it in some shape. I resumed male attire at the earliest possible moment and figured once more as Lieutenant Harry T. Buford.

The war had now been in progress for nearly two years. Although the South had not been conquered, affairs were beginning to look decidedly blue for us. The country was becoming exhausted, the cultivation of the ground was neglected, and the necessities of life every day became scarcer and dearer. The suffering among the poorer classes in all parts of the South was very great. Many of the people were very nearly on the verge of starvation.

I resolved to abandon the West, for the present at least. I thought that in Virginia I would be likely to have a better chance for distinguishing myself, I felt certain that a skillful spy, such as I esteemed myself to be, could find out plenty of things which the Richmond authorities would be glad to know The military situation in Virginia, too, was more satisfactory than it was in the West, and I had a hankering to be where the Confederates were occasionally winning some victories.

Richmond, however, was a very different place from what it was on my last visit to it, as I soon found to my cost. Martial law was in force in its most rigorous aspect and General Winder, the chief of the secret service bureau, and his emissaries, were objects of terror to everybody, rich and poor. Strangers were watched with a vigilance that left them few opportunities to do mischief or were put under arrest if Winder or his officers took it that this would be the most expeditious way of disposing of them.

It is not surprising that almost immediately upon my arrival in Richmond I fell under the surveillance of Winder as a suspicious character. I was arrested on the charge of being a woman in disguise and supposably a Federal spy and was conducted to Castle Thunder till I could give a satisfactory account of myself. But good luck often comes to us in the guise of present tribulation. As matters turned out, it was the very best thing that could have happened to me, for it compelled me to reveal myself and to tell my story to friendly and sympathetic ears.

The commander of Castle Thunder was Major G.W. Alexander. Major Alexander and his lovely wife both treated me with such kindness and consideration that I was induced to tell them exactly who I was. They not only believed my story but, thinking that my services to the Confederacy merited better treatment than I was receiving, undertook to represent my case to General Winder. General Winder ordered my release and assigned me a position in the secret service corps.

General Winder was one of the most remarkable men I became acquainted with during my whole career in the Confederate service. He was a venerable, pleasant-looking old gentleman with white hair and a rather agreeable countenance. He had a most confiding, plausible way about him and an air of general benevolence that completely masked the hardness of his heart. He imposed so on his victims that, until they found themselves fairly caught in his cunningly-laid traps, they were unwilling to believe him the desperate old sinner he really was. I do not believe that the man had such a thing as a conscience; he was utterly unscrupulous with regard to the means he took to accomplish his ends. I doubt whether another individual in the whole Confederacy could have been found who would have commanded the secret service corps with the signal ability he did.

Such was the new commander under whom I was now to go on duty, and who, when he consented to release me from prison and give me employment, prepared as pretty a trap as was ever devised for catching an innocent. The trap was sprung in first-rate style, but the intended victim was agile enough to slip through the wires; the result was that General Winder gained nothing but his trouble for his pains. I had unlimited confidence in my own abilities and accepted the commission he gave me as a secret service agent with a determination to carry out my instructions to the letter. General Winder started me out with despatches for General Earl Van Dorn. The despatches were simply a lot of blank papers and a letter explaining the little game Winder was playing with me.

Unsuspicious of any evil intentions on the part of the white-headed, benevolent-looking old gentleman, I hastened to execute my orders. Winder had telegraphed to the

Lt. Buford meets General Winder.

provost marshal at Charlotte, N.C., to have me arrested. When the train stopped at that place, a gawky member of the North Carolina home-guard took me into custody and demanded the papers I had in my pocket. It now flashed upon me that Winder had put up a job on me and I resolved that he should not have the satisfaction of succeeding.

I measured my captor with my eye and saw at a glance that he was not the brightest-witted specimen ever created; if I only put on enough dignity I would have no difficulty getting the best of him. It was evidently somewhat of a novelty for the tar-heeled home-guarder to arrest an officer. While he felt the importance of the occasion immensely, he was in some degree of trepidation, especially when he saw that I was not disposed to acknowledge his authority.

I refused to give up the papers and demanded in the severest manner I could command what right he had to arrest a Confederate officer travelling under orders. He showed me his orders, which I was forced to acknowledge were correct, but still declined to either give up the papers or submit to an arrest. I promptly offered to return to Richmond with them, and report at headquarters to General Winder.

This completely nonplussed him, and he was in a terrible quandary. I pitied the poor fellow's perplexity, but could scarcely help from laughing in his face at his desperate stupidity. He blinked his eyes at a terrible rate and great drops of sweat oozed from his forehead, which he wiped off with the sleeve of his jacket as he tried to argue with me. I would not give in in the least, and seeing that he did not have the slightest comprehension of the duties of his office, I suggested that a telegraph should be sent back to headquarters asking for further instructions. This settled the case; I was released and was soon on my way again.

I finally reached General Van Dorn, to whom I delivered my package of supposed despatches. He read Winder's letter and looked through the lot of blanks which had accompanied it; then, glancing at me, he burst into a laugh which indicated he saw something funny in the proceeding. After a few questions, he ordered me to return. I did not particularly admire having been sent all this distance on a fool's errand and was very much disposed to resent it. A little reflection, however, told me that I had accomplished my errand according to order without falling into the snare that General Winder had set for me. I had every reason to be satisfied and would probably find that he was satisfied also.

Chapter Fifteen

In the summer of 1863, General Lee had invaded Pennsylvania, had been defeated at Gettysburg, and had returned to Virginia to resume the defense of Richmond. The attention of the entire Confederacy was now anxiously directed to Eastern Tennessee, where the Federal General Rosecrans was pushing forward with the evident intention of forcing his way into Georgia. It was in resisting Rosecrans, therefore, that distinction was to be won, not by remaining in Richmond. As I always liked to be where the heaviest fighting was going on, I concluded that I ought to set my face southward if I hoped to win any laurels.

On reaching Atlanta, I had the gratification of receiving letters from relatives from whom I had not heard for many months. This was the first time in nine months I had heard from my brother and the first intimation I had that he was in the army. I was well pleased to learn that he was in the Confederate Service, but I was glad that he was so far off that

CHARLOTTE STATION

Detained by the Home Guard

there was not much danger of my meeting him. I felt certain he would object to my assuming male attire for the purpose of doing a share of the fighting and feared that we might quarrel about it.

Shortly after my arrival in Atlanta, I heard something that delighted me even more than the letters. This was that Captain De Caulp was near Spring Hill with Van Dorn. I was seized with an intense desire to meet him again, for I was greatly in love with him, and it afforded me the keenest delight to hear praises of myself from his lips, and he all the while thinking he was addressing them to a third party. To have been able to fight by the side of my lover in one of the greatest battles of the war and to be praised by him for my valor were of themselves matters for intense satisfaction; I often imagined how, after the war was over, we would be able to compare notes and relate our adventures to each other.

I was almost more than half resolved to give him a surprise by revealing myself to him. Whether to do this or not was a question I debated with myself while on my way to join him. The fact that I was a woman had now been so often discovered, that it was probable he might at any moment learn that his expected wife and Lieutenant Harry T. Buford were one and the same. Not knowing what he might think of the course I had pursued in assuming male attire, I dreaded having anyone but myself reveal my secret to him. I knew that, in many respects, it would be better for me to remain at a distance from Captain De Caulp, but I was moved by an inscrutable impulse to go to him.

So, as soon as I found that Captain De Caulp was near at hand, I took the train for the point where Van Dorn's command was stationed. Getting off at Tyner's Station, I obtained a horse and started off in the direction of Chickamauga. I fell in with General Pegram's cavalry and learned that it would be almost impossible to reach Van Dorn. I met some officers and men of the tenth Tennessee regiment, from whom I obtained some ideas which induced me to make some rather different plans from those which I had been endeavoring to carry out.

Chapter Sixteen

The position and duties of spies are little understood by persons who have had no actual experience of warfare. Just as the quartermaster, the commissary, the paymaster and the surgeon are as important as the generals, so the spy, who will obtain information of the movements of the enemy; who will discover the plans for battles and campaigns; who will prove himself prompt and dependable in taking any fact worth knowing to headquarters, is indispensable to the success of any movement.

The spy, however, occupies a different position from that held by any other attach of an army. According to all military law he is an outlaw, liable to be hung if detected. Nothing has been left undone to render the labors of the spy not only perilous in the extreme, but infamous. And yet the spy is nothing more nor less than a detective officer, and there cannot be any good reason for the discredit which attaches to his profession. Having been for a long period a spy myself, and a very successful one, I feel no compunction in relating a number of transactions which, at first sight, the reader may think were not to my credit. All I ask is that fair-minded persons remember that the circumstances were not ordinary ones. I was mixed up in a good deal of rascally business, but it was my associates and not myself who were deserving of condemnation. I even now shudder to think of the

Lt. Buford falls in with Pegram's Cavalry.

depravities of human nature which my career as a secret agent of the Confederate government revealed to me.

But it will be enough to speak of these things when the proper time comes. My special task just now is to relate the prosecution of my adventures. It appeared to be more trouble than it was worth to persuade any of the general officers to assign me to the particular kind of duty I desired. As I had been decidedly successful in more than one expedition planned and executed by myself on my own responsibility, I resolved to undertake another one, just for the sake of keeping myself busy and of seeing what would come of it.

My idea now was to run through the lines, and take a good view of the situation from the Federal standpoint. I knew that the safest and best way of doing this - if, indeed, not the only one - was to go as a woman. The only difficulty in the way of accomplishing my objective was in procuring suitable clothing without attracting attention. As there were a number of houses in the vicinity from which the people had fled when they found themselves in the midst of contending armies, it occurred to me that I would be able to find what I wanted in one of them.

I commenced a search and soon came to a dwelling that promised to supply me with eveything I needed. I forced my way in through one of the back windows. Sure enough, I found an abundance of female clothing to select from and proceeded to appropriate the best outfit the wardrobe of the absent mistress of the establishment afforded. As she must be a good Confederate, she would highly approve of my conduct, could she be informed of the use to which her dresses and underwear were being put.

Having transformed myself from a gallant young Confederate officer into a reasonably good-looking woman, I packed a carpetbag with a change of clothing and other articles I thought might be useful on a journey. My uniform I folded up carefully and put into a pillowcase. I put the pillowcase into an ash-barrel and, covering it with ashes, placed it in a corner where it would not attract attention. I succeeded in making a tolerably hearty meal by eating some raw ham and all the preserves I could find. I then picked up my carpetbag and made directly for the enemy's lines.

I knew that the bold way was the best way in the execution of such an enterprise as that upon which I was now starting. The correct plan was to strike directly for headquarters with a plausible story to tell, rather than to attempt to slip past the pickets and run the risk of being detected. Until actually within the Federal lines, however, I would be, so to speak, between two fires and would stand a chance of being used quite as roughly by my friends as by the enemy. It was important, therefore, for me to make the distance I had to go as quickly as I could and yet to avoid appearing in too much of a hurry, in case anyone should happen to see me.

The dangers attending the enterprise gave it a certain pleasurable excitement, such as it otherwise would not have had and I enjoyed it, after a fashion, immensely - even more than I did the excitement of battle. Luckily for me no one observed my movements and I made my way to the nearest Federal picket station without interruption. I gave my name as Mrs. Williams, told as much as I thought the officer in charge ought to know about me, and asked to see General Rosecrans. I was accordingly ushered into the general's presence and gave him a somewhat more detailed account of myself.

I represented that I was a widow who was endeavoring to escape from the Confederacy and go to friends in the North. He asked me a great number of questions, which I

Finding women's clothing in an abandoned home

answered to his satisfaction, then dismissed me with a pass permitting me to go North. I could not help smiling at the ease with which I deceived General Rosecrans and said to myself as I retired from his presence, "My good fellow, I'll teach you what we Southern women are good for before I am done with you."

Having got my pass, I started off with a notion of seeing all I could see and finding out all I could find out, watching all the time for an opportunity for the execution of a grand coup. I travelled as far as Martinsburg and had a notion of proceeding to Washington, to see whether a second visit to that city might not be even more productive than my first. Circumstances occurred, however, which detained me in Martinsburg and my trip to Washington, therefore, was deferred to another opportunity.

It was after night when I reached Martinsburg, and the only unoccupied room in the hotel was one belonging to the Federal quartermaster, who had been called away to Washington. The landlord put me in there, and I proceeded to make myself as much at home as possible. As luck would have it, however, the officer returned during the night, after I had retired; finding the door bolted, he commenced a furious knocking. I was asleep when he began to make this noise. I thought some drunken fellow was making a disturbance and that when he found he could not get in he would go away. The quartermaster, however, was angry at finding his room occupied, and finally said, "Open the door inside there, or I will break it open!"

I thought it was high time for me to speak now, and so said in a half terrified tone of voice, "Who are you? What do you want?"

Finding that his apartment had a feminine occupant, he lowered his voice, said, "Excuse me, madam," and walked to the office, where he gave the clerk some sharp words for permitting anyone to take his room. I heard him say, "I would like thundering well to know who she is," but the clerk was unable to give him any information and he was obliged to sleep in the parlor.

The next morning, I overheard the quartermaster say to the old porter, "Do you know who that woman is that they put in my room last night? Is she good looking?"

"She's a pretty good looking lady."

This was flattering and served to give me a hint to the kind of man I had to deal with in the quartermaster. Having made my morning toilet and having endeavored to make myself as attractive as possible, I went and took a seat in the parlor. It was not long before I saw my gentleman walking past the door, looking at me with a rather curious gaze. I took no notice of him, concluding that it would be more to the purpose to let him make the first advances, something that he was evidently not indisposed to do.

Breakfast was announced and with the announcement came the quartermaster's opportunity to introduce himself. He bowed politely and said, "Are you Mrs. Williams?"

"Yes, sir." I replied. "That is my name."

"I owe you an apology, madam, for the disturbance I made last night. I was not aware there was a lady in the room."

"O, sir," I said, "no apology is necessary. Indeed, I owe you one, for I must have caused you some inconvenience."

"Not at all, madam. I regretted exceedingly that I made so much noise. We officers are inclined to become rather rough in our ways, owing to our absence from female society. We forget sometimes how to behave ourselves."

"O, pray, sir, don't apologize," I answered. "I am sure that an officer of our brave army would not be intentionally rude under any circumstances." I thought this would do to start the idea in his mind that I was a staunch Federal.

During the meal my friend manifested the greatest interest in me and my movements. By a series of questions he elicited the information that I was from Cincinnati, that I was uncertain how long I would remain, and that I was in search of a brother, who I feared was either killed or wounded, as he had not been heard of for a long time.

While making the journey to Martinsburg, I had accumulated an extensive stock of knowledge which I thought might be useful at some time. Among other things, I had learned the name of a Federal soldier belonging to General Averill's command and made a mental note of it for future reference. My friend asked me what company my brother belonged to. I said I could not tell him that. All I knew was that he was under Averill and that, as the command had been engaged in some sharp fighting lately, his family were becoming exceedingly anxious.

I wiped the semblance of a tear from my eye as I said this and looked as distressed as possible. The quartermaster proved as sympathetic as I could have desired and promised to find out where my brother was, if he was still alive, or if he had been killed. When we had finished breakfast, he went immediately to headquarters to inspect the roll of the command. Before a great while he returned and, with a sorrowful countenance, stated that it gave him pain to tell me that my dear brother was dead.

"O, that is awful!" I cried, actually squeezing out a few real tears.

My friend tried to soothe me as well as he could. Finally, becoming calm, I asked him where Dick was buried and declared that I must visit his grave. He said he would get an ambulance and take me to the burial place.

Before many moments, my friend and I drove out to where my supposed brother was buried. It was now my turn to question and my escort proved to be so communicative that before we returned to the hotel I was informed of the exact number of troops in the neighborhood, their positions, their commanders, the results of the recent conflicts and a variety of other matters. The man was as innocent as a newborn babe. I could scarcely keep from laughing at the eagerness he displayed in telling me things that, had he been possessed of ordinary common sense, he would never have revealed to anyone.

Some of the information I knew would be of vital importance to the Confederates. I therefore made my arrangement, and that night slipped through the Federal lines, and told all that I had to one of Mosby's pickets. I succeeded in getting back without being observed or suspected and my escort of the morning was never the wiser.

I remained a week in Martinsburg and enjoyed myself immensely. This week was not an idle one; by the time it was ended I was in possession of a large number of facts that were well worth knowing. When I announced that I was about to depart, the officers expressed the greatest regret. The quartermaster insisted that I should write to him when I got home. I gave him a pressing invitation to come and see me when the war was over, thinking that he would have a good time in finding me.

When I got back to Chattanooga, I had some trouble making further progress. My anxiety now was to regain the Confederate lines at the earliest possible moment. Fortune favors the brave, and ere long I was able to reach the farmhouse where I had left my uniform, only to find that it had been burned. To my great joy, however, I discovered the ash-

Visiting her "brother's" grave

barrel unharmed and in a few moments I was once more in the guise of a Confederate officer. Ere many moments I was crawling through the underbrush and under the fences with my coat and cap tied in a bundle. In this way I worked myself slowly along for several hours during the night. When it was light enough for me to see I concluded that I must have been within the Confederate lines for more than an hour.

Drawing on my coat, I began to think what story it would be best to tell in order to obtain such a reception as I desired. I concluded to represent myself as an escaped prisoner belonging to Morgan's command. I walked up boldly to a picket and asked to see the officer of the guard. The officer scanned me very closely, as if he thought there was something not quite right about me. I, however, bore his scrutiny without flinching. I pulled out a little pocket flask of whiskey and asked him if he would take a drink. His eyes brightened at the sight of the flask and he accepted my invitation without a moment's hesitation. The whiskey had the desired effect, for the officer told me I had better not wait for the relief, and detailed a man to show me the way to camp.

On our arrival at camp, I was speedily surrounded by a crowd of eager questioners who were anxious to hear all the news from the Federal army. I told them that the Yankees had received heavy reinforcements and were preparing to make a grand movement and other matters, part fact and part fiction. I took a quick sleep until noon and then, borrowing a horse, rode to Dalton where I learned that Captain De Caulp was sick at Atlanta, and resolved to get there to see him.

I was spared the necessity of making any plans for the accomplishment of this end when I managed to severely hurt the foot which had been wounded shortly after the battle at Fort Donelson, and it was decided to send me to Atlanta for treatment.

Chapter Eighteen

On my arrival at Atlanta, I went to the hotel and registered. I was almost immediately surrounded by a number of officers who were eager to learn what was going on at the front. Among them was General F. (I do not give his name in full for his own sake), an individual who thought more of whiskey than he did of his future existence and who was employing his time in getting drunk at Atlanta instead of doing his duty at the front leading his men. He saw that I was a little fellow and probably thought on that account he could bully me with impunity.

He began making offensive and insulting remarks and asking me insolent questions until I longed to give him a lesson in good manners. As I neither wished to be annoyed by his drunken insolence nor to quarrel with him if I could avoid it, I went into the washroom. The general followed me, apparently determined to provoke me to the utmost. I took no notice of him, but, after washing my hands, came out and took a seat in the office.

My persecutor now came and seated himself on the other side of me and made some insolent remark - which I do not care to remember. This excited my wrath and I said to him, "See here, sir, I don't want to have anything to do with you, so go away and let me be, or it will be worse for you."

At this he sprang up, his eyes glaring with drunken fury; swinging his arms around, he began to swear in a lively fashion and said, "What'll be worse for me? I'll lick you out of your boots! I can lick you, or any dozen like you."

"You are too drunk, sir, to be responsible," I merely said in reply. "I intend, when you are sober, that you shall apologize to me for this, or else make you settle it in a way that will not be agreeable to you."

He glared at me as I uttered these words; but my firm manner evidently cowed him. Turning with a coarse, tipsy laugh, he said to an officer who was standing near, "Come, colonel, let's take another drink; he won't fight."

The general did not come near me again until after supper. As I had not undertaken to punish him for his behavior, he evidently thought I was afraid of him. Without addressing me directly, he began making insulting remarks aimed at me. I was on the point of slapping his face when Major Bacon and Lieutenant Chamberlain, thinking it was not worthwhile for me to trouble about such a fellow, induced me to go to my room. Already quite ill, the excitement of this unpleasant occurrence made me worse and I passed a night of great suffering from high fever and from my sore foot, which pained me extremely. It was concluded that the hospital was the best place for me and I was sent to the Empire Hospital by order of the chief surgeon of the post.

O, but these were sad and weary days that I spent in the hospital! I cannot tell how I longed to be out in the open air and sunshine, participating in the grand scenes that were being enacted not many miles away. There was one consolation, however, in all my sufferings - I was near the man I loved, and hoped soon to see and converse with him. I resolved that if Captain De Caulp was willing, our marriage should take place so soon as we were able to leave the hospital. I busied myself in wondering what he would say when he discovered what strange pranks I had been playing since we had been corresponding as lovers. There was nothing that I had done that I need blush for, while he had himself been the witness, on one momentous occasion, of my prowess as a warrior. I longed to hear him repeat to me, as a woman, the praise he had so freely bestowed upon me as a man when we fought side by side at Shiloh.

After a weary waiting, which I thought would never end, both Captain De Caulp and myself were convalescent. At the earliest moment that I could obtain permission to leave my ward I went to see him. He was extremely glad to see me, much more so than I had expected. He smiled and held out his hand and said, "I am mighty glad to see you again, lieutenant. It is like meeting a brother."

After some little preliminary talk I said, "Captain, are you married yet? You told me you were engaged and were expecting to ask the lady to name the day."

"No," said he, "the wedding has not come off yet, but I hope it will very shortly. This spell of sickness has knocked all my plans in the head."

"Does the lady know that you are sick?"

"I doubt whether she does," he replied. "The last letter I had stated that she would meet me here, but for several months I have been unable to communicate with her." He then took the letter he referred to out of a package, evidently made up of my epistles, and read it to me. He also showed me a picture of myself and handed it to me, saying, "That is the woman I love, what do you think of her?"

This was almost too much for me. All trembling with emotion, I handed it back to him, saying, "She is a fine-looking woman."

"Yes," said he, "and she is just as good as she is good-looking. I think the world of her and want to see her again - O, so badly!"

"Have you known her for long, Captain?" I asked with a trembling voice, scarcely daring to trust myself to speak. I turned away and wiped the tears from my eyes and attempted to recover my composure before I confronted him again.

"Yes," he said. "She is a widow, and her husband was an excellent friend of mine. Why, you ought to know her. Her husband was the first captain of our company. You recollect him, surely."

"Yes, I have had a slight acquaintance with her, but you probably have known her longer than I have. When did you see her last?"

"I have not seen her for three years," he replied.

"Have you been engaged to her that long?"

"O, no. I did not become engaged to her until about six months after the death of her husband. We had some correspondence about the settlement of his affairs and we kept on writing to each other after these were arranged. I thought she was a first-rate woman, the kind that you don't meet every day. After about six months I asked her to marry me and she accepted me without hesitation."

"What would you give if you could see your lady now?" I asked in a voice so choked with emotion I could barely utter these words.

"O, I would almost give my existence in heaven."

I could not bear to hear any more. I made a hasty excuse and left the room so abruptly that he must have seen there was something the matter with me.

The next morning I wrote him a note in my proper person, stating that I had arrived and was coming to see him. Burning with anxiety to see what the effect of the letter would be, I followed hard upon the bearer and passed by the door in such a manner that he could not fail to see me. "Lieutenant, come in," he called out. Holding out the note, which I had written but a few moments before, he said, with the happiest smile I ever saw on a human face, "She has come; she has come and will be here soon. Congratulate me, my friend."

"Captain, I congratulate you heartily, and I hope to have the pleasure of meeting your lady. As you doubtless want to talk over a number of confidential matters, don't you think it would be better if the doctor were to move you into a private room?"

"Yes, that is just what I would like. Tell the doctor I want to see him."

The doctor cheerfully granted his request and had him taken to a private chamber. A barber was then sent for and he was shaved and made to look as nice as possible. It touched me deeply to notice what pains he took to make himself presentable in view of the expected arrival of his lady-love. I said gravely, "Now, captain, I have something of great importance to say to you before your sweetheart comes."

I knelt by the bedside, and taking from my a pocket a picture of himself that he had sent me, and his last letter, said, "Did you ever see these before?"

He glanced at them and turned deathly pale. "Yes, they are mine. Where did you get them? Has anything happened?"

"No, no, captain," I exclaimed. "You must not be frightened. Nothing has happened that will be displeasing to you. You told me last night, when you showed me the portrait of your lady, that you had not seen her for three years. Are you so very sure of that?"

He looked at the picture, and then at me, with a most puzzled expression until I said, "Well, captain, don't you think that the picture of your lady-love looks the least bit like your friend Harry Buford?"

71

Loreta and Captain De Caulp are reunited.

A light seemed to suddenly break upon him; he gasped for breath and sank back on his pilllow, great drops of perspiration standing out all over his forehead. Then, raising himself, he looked me hard in the face and, grasping my hand tightly, exclaimed, "Can it be possible that you are she?"

"Yes," said I, clasping his hand still tighter. "I am, indeed, your own Loreta. It was your sweetheart who fought by your side at the great battle of Shiloh; and not only on that occasion, but ever since the outbreak of the war, she has been doing a soldier's work for the cause of the Confederacy. Can you love her a little for that as well as for herself?"

"I love you ten times more than ever for this, Loreta!" he said, with a vehemence that brought tears of joy to my eyes.

I then went into a long explanation of my reasons for acting as I had done and gave him an outline of my adventures, reserving the details for a time when he would be stronger and less agitated. He then burst into tears and, leaning his face on my shoulder said, between sobs, "O, Loreta, can it be possible that you have been so far from me, and yet so near to me all this time?"

To say that I was supremely happy but faintly expresses what I felt as I left the chamber of Captain De Caulp. It all seemed like a dream to me, but it was a happy one and I desired never to awaken from it. I was of too practical a disposition, however, to give way to mere sentiment on such an occasion as this. The fact that my lover was still confined to a sickbed rendered it the more important that I should be about and making such preparations as were necessary for our approaching marriage.

I was anxious that the affair should pass off as quietly as possible and particularly desired not to give any opportunity for unseemly gossip or talk. I procured a sufficiency of women's apparel for my wedding outfit by purchasing clothing at a variety of places under the pleas that I wanted the garments for some persons out of town, or for presents to the girls at the hotel - whatever story I thought would serve my purpose. We both concluded that a very modest wardrobe would be all I would need, the main thing being that I should be dressed as a woman when the ceremony took place for fear of making the clergyman feel unpleasant, should I appear before him hanging on the captain's arm in my uniform.

My arrangements having all been made, we concluded to inform the friends whom we had agreed to invite. The next day Captain De Caulp and I were married in the parlor of the hotel by the post chaplain in as quiet and unpretentious a way as either of us could desire. Our kind friends wished us all manner of happiness, and we both looked forward to a bright future when, after the war was over, we could settle down in our home, and enjoy the blessings of peace in each other's society.

I was very desirous of resuming my uniform and accompanying my husband to the field. I wanted to go through the war with him and to fight by his side, just as I had done at Shiloh. He, however, was bitterly opposed to this; and, with ample knowledge of army life, I could not but admit the full force of his objections. I very reluctantly yielded to his wishes although, if I could have looked a little into the future, I either would have prevented his going to the front at all or else would have insisted upon going with him.

Our honeymoon was a very brief one. In about a week he thought himself well enough to report for duty; and he insisted upon going, notwithstanding my entreaties for him to remain until his health was more robust. When I found that further argument would be useless, I prepared his baggage and bade him a sorrowful adieu.

Loreta and Captain De Caulp are married.

Before reaching his command, Captain De Caulp was taken sick again. Before I obtained any information of his condition, he had died in a Federal hospital in Chattanooga. This was a terrible blow to me, for I tenderly loved my husband and was greatly beloved by him. Our short married life was a very happy one. Its sudden ending brought to naught the pleasant plans I had for the future, and left me nothing to do but launch once more on a life of adventure and to devote my energies to the Confederate cause.

Chapter Nineteen

The military situation at this time—the fall of 1863—was of painful interest, and the fate of the Confederacy seemed to hang trembling in the balance. In Virginia, General Lee was defending Richmond with all his old success, and was holding one immense army in check so effectively that the prospect of entering the Confederate capital as conquerors must have seemed to the enemy more remote than ever. In the West and South, however, the Confederates had lost much, and the question now was whether they would be able to hold what they had until the Federals were exhausted, or until England and France consented to aid by recognizing the Confederacy and perhaps by armed intervention.

It was at Richmond and at Chattanooga that the contending forces were massed, although there was plenty of fighting going on elsewhere, and some of these minor campaigns were of great importance and did much to enable the Confederacy to prolong the contest for nearly eighteen months. I started for Richmond for the purpose of making a definite offer of my service to the Confederate authorities there. Bad as the condition of things was, I was in a more hopeful frame of mind than I had been for a long time and I was anxious to labor, as I felt I was able to labor, in behalf of the cause.

With only the most indefinite plans for the future, I proceeded on my arrival in Richmond to call on General Winder and to procure an interview with President Davis. Mr. Davis was opposed to permitting me to serve in the army as an officer, attired in male costume, while he had no duties to which he could properly assign me as a woman. I returned to General Winder, but got little encouragement from him. He finally consented to give me a letter of recommendation to the commanding officer of the forces in the South and West. This was better than nothing, and I thought that I could scarcely fail to accomplish something of value to the cause.

I started off and, for the last time, made a grand tour of the entire Southern Confederacy. Stopping from point to point, I gathered all the information I could, and endeavored to find a place where I could commence active operations with the best chance of achieving something of importance. During the course of the long journey, however, I failed to meet with the grand opportunity I sighed for until I fiinally reached Mobile.

In Mobile I met quite a number of officers whom I had met on various battlefields, and received the kindest and best attentions from them. The flattering commendations that were bestowed upon me served to mitigate the disappointment I felt on account of the non-recognition of my services in other quarters.

Shortly after my arrival at Mobile, I received a rather mysterious note in a masculine hand, asking me to meet the writer that evening at the corner of the square, but giving no hint whatever of the purpose of the invitation. I hesitated for some time about taking any notice of the request, thinking that if the writer had any real business with me, he would

President Jefferson Davis opposes Loreta's serving as a Confederate officer or spy.

communicate with me in a less mysterious way. The fact, however, that I was travelling under credentials from General Winder, and was in a manner an attach of the Secret Service Department, rendered it not improbable that this was an application for me to undertake some such enterprise as I for a long time had been ardently desirous of engaging in.

My surmise proved to be correct. I had scarcely arrived at the corner of the square when my correspondent, who I discovered was Lieutenant Shorter, of Arkansas, advanced toward me and said, "Good evening. I am glad to see you. How have you been?"

"I am quite well," I replied.

After a few inconsequential remarks on either side he said, "I see that you received my note."

"Yes."

"You have had considerable experience in running through the lines, and in spy and secret service duty, have you not?"

"Yes," I replied. "I have done something in that line."

"You have usually been tolerably lucky, haven't you?"

"Yes, I have had reasonably good luck. I got caught once in New Orleans, but that was because the parties to whom I had delivered my despatches were captured; I managed to slip away before there was any postive evidence against me."

"Well, you're just the kind I want, for I have a job on hand that will require both skill and nerve. I am in the secret service, and I want you to take a dispatch through the lines. Meet me tomorrow evening at Meridian. I will have everything ready for you."

We then said good night and parted, I going back to the hotel to do a heap of thinking before I went to sleep. I concluded to procure a very plain suit of women's clothing and to make up a small bundle of articles I thought I would require. I started for Meridian the next day and found Lieutenant Shorter waiting for me at the depot. I was far from being well and felt that I was scarcely doing either myself or the others justice in undertaking such an enterprise, under liability that I might be taken seriously sick before concluding it. I had great confidence, however, in my power of will. Having promised Lieutenant Shorter that I would go, I was determined to do so.

The lieutenant said he had captured a spy belonging to Federal General Hurlbut's command, and had taken from him a paper containing quite accurate accounts of the forces of Chalmers, Forrest, Richardson, and Ferguson and their movements. This he had changed so that it would throw the enemy on the wrong scent; I was to take it to Memphis to Federal General Washburn and induce him to believe that I had obtained it from the spy. He also had a despatch for Forrest, which he wanted me to take to the Confederate secret agent in Memphis, telling me where to find him and giving me the password which would enable me to communicate with him without difficulty.

After some further conversation about the plan, Lieutenant Shorter suggested some changes in my dress, his idea being that I should personate a poor countrywoman who had lost her husband at the start of the war, and who was flying into the Federal lines for protection. He also gave me letters to the various Confederate commanders whom I would meet on my road, directing them to assist me, and put in my hand the sum of one hundred and thirty-six dollars which had been taken from the captured spy. This, he thought, would see me through; but in case it should not prove sufficient, he said that any commanding officer I met would supply me with funds. After I reached Memphis I would find plenty of friends of the Confederacy upon whom I could call for assistance.

Chapter Twenty

The next morning I took the train for Okolona, and drove to the headquarters of General Ferguson. The general received me with the greatest politeness and gave me additional instructions. He handed me ninety dollars and a pistol, one of a pair he had carried through the war. The money he was sure I would need and the pistol might be a handy thing to have, for my journey would take me through rough country. He advised me not to use the weapon except in case of absolute necessity and especially not to carry it with me into the Federal lines, for it might excite suspicions that I was a spy.

A fine horse having been provided for me, I said adieu to General Ferguson and started off with an escort to conduct me to a point somewhere to the northeast of Holly Springs. In spite of the fact that I was quite sick and sometimes felt that I could scarcely sit upon my horse, I rode all that night and nearly all the next day—through lonesome woods, past desolate clearings, occupied by poor negroes or even poorer whites, all of whom had a half-terrified look, as if they were expecting every moment to have a rapacious soldiery come tramping through their little patches of ground,—through gullies and ravines and over the roughest kind of roads or sometimes no road at all. At length we reached a cabin which, although a poor shelter, was better than nothing at all. Feeling too ill to proceed any further without rest and refreshments, I resolved to stop there all night.

The inhabitants of the cabin apparently did not want me for a lodger and their abode was not one I would have cared to make a prolonged sojourn in. I was too much of a veteran, however, to be over-fastidious about my accomodation for a single night and was too sick not to find any shelter welcome. I secured their good will by promising to pay well for my night's lodging and finally succeeded in inducing them to make me as comfortable as circumstances would permit. I also struck up a bargain with an old man who appeared to be the head of the household to act as a guide in the morning. Then, completely used up by my long and toilsome ride, I retired to the miserable bed that was assigned me and, ere long, was in happy obliviousness of the cares and trials of this world.

About three o'clock in the morning I was up and ready to start. Through woods, over fields, along rough county roads, making shortcuts wherever we saw a chance to do so, we pursued our way for several hours duing the damp and dismal gray morning twilight. Our journey continued without interruption until, at length, I spied through the trees a little church. It was now broad daylight, although the sun was not yet up.

I surmised, from what my guide had told me, that the Federal pickets must be somewhere near. I rode up to the church and entered the building. My first care now was to get rid of my pistol. Raising a plank in the flooring, I put the pistol under it and covered it well with dirt. My intention was to return this way and I expected to get the weapon and give it back to General Ferguson. Circumstances, however, induced me to change my plans. As I have never visited the spot since, if the church is still standing, the pistol is probably still where I placed it for I buried it tolerably deep.

Having ascertained that my papers were all right, I mounted my pony again and started in the direction of the Federal camp. Letting my pony take his own gait, I travelled for a couple of miles before I saw anyone. At length a picket stepped out of the woods into the road, halted me, and asked me where I was from and where I was going.

"Good morning, sir," I said in an innocent, unsophisticated sort of way. "Are you commanding this outpost?"

Loreta is stopped by a Yankee picket.

"No," he replied, "what do you want?"

"Well, sir, I wish you would tell the captain I want to see him."

"What do you want with the captain?"

"I have a message to give the captain. I can't give it to anyone else."

"He is over there in the woods."

"Well, you just tell him that I want to see him quick, about something very important."

The soldier then called his officer. As he approached me, he tipped his hat with a pleasant smile. "Good morning, madam. What is it you wish?"

"Well, captain," said I. "I want to go to Memphis to see General Washburn. I have some papers here for him."

This made him start a little. He began to suspect that he had a matter of serious business on hand. He inquired, with a rather severe and serious air, "Where are you from, madam?"

"I am from Holly Springs. A man there gave me these papers and told me that if I could get them through he would pay me a hundred dollars."

"What kind of man was he? Where did he go after he left you?"

"I mustn't tell you that, sir. The man said not to tell anything about him, except to the one these papers are for, and he would understand all about it.

"Well, madam, you will have to go with me to headquarters."

The lieutenant took me to Moscow, on the Memphis and Charleston Railroad. Here, for the first time, I was subjected to serious annoyance and first began to appreciate that I was engaged in a particularly risky undertaking. The soldiers, seeing me coming into town on a ragged little pony and under the escort of an officer, jumped at the conclusion that I was a spy, and commenced to gather around me in crowds.

"Who is she?" someone asked.

"O, she's a spy that the Illinois picket captured."

"You're gone up!" yelled some fellow in the crowd.

"Why don't they hang her?" was the pleasant inquiry of another.

Some of the brutal fellows pushed against me and struck my pony and otherwise made my progress exceedingly unpleasant. Finally we reached the building occupied by the colonel in command. The lieutenant related the manner of my coming to the picket station, and the story which I had told him.

The colonel then proceeded to cross-examine me. I flattered myself that I played my part tolerably well. I stuck close to one simple story. I was a poor widow woman. I was for the Union and had been badly treated by the rebels, who had robbed me of nearly everything. I had been anxious to get away with a little money I had collected, and had finally got tired of waiting for the Federal troops to come down my way, and had resolved to get through the lines. A man had promised I should be paid a hundred dollars if I would carry a despatch to General Washburn. I was to deliver the papers to General Washburn only and was to tell him alone certain things that the man had told me. I hoped that General Washburn, after I had given the despatch to him, would pay me the hundred dollars and furnish me with a pass to go North.

The colonel was tolerably smart at cross-examination, but not by any means smart enough for the subject he had to deal with on this occasion. I had the most innocent air about me, and pretended that I was so stupid that I could not understand what his inquiries meant, and, instead of answering them, would go off into a long story about my troubles and hardships. The colonel tried to induce me to give him the despatch, saying that he would pay me the hundred dollars and would forward it to General Washburn. This I refused to do. Neither would I tell who had entrusted me with it or give any clue to the message for the general he had entrusted me to deliver by word of mouth.

Finding that no information worth talking about was to be obtained from me, he said, "Where will you go if I give you a pass?"

"I want to go to Memphis, sir, to give this paper to General Washburn. I hope the general will be kind enough to send me to Ohio"

"Have you any money?"

"Yes, sir, about one hundred and fifty dollars."

"Confederate money, isn't it?"

"No, sir. It's greenbacks. I wouldn't have that rebel trash; it isn't worth anything."

"Well, madam," said the colonel, "remain here until the train is ready and I will see what I can do for you."

The train came in at one o'clock and I proceeded to the depot under the escort of the two officers. The colonel procured me a ticket and gave me five dollars. I overheard him say in an undertone to the lieutenant, "Keep an eye on her. I think she is all right, but it would be just as well to watch her."

The lieutenant said, "O, there's no doubt in my mind but she is all right."

This little conversation made me smile to myself and served to convince me that I would have no trouble getting along nicely with my friend the lieutenant. The colonel moved off and the lieutenant and I stepped aboard the train with a half dozen soldiers who were nearby making such comments as, "I guess she'll hang," and "Hanging's too good for a spy." The lieutenant was overwhelmingly polite. After having got me fixed comfortably in my seat, he said in a low tone, "I may go up with you as far as my camp, if I can get anyone to hold my horse."

"O, I would be so glad if you would. I would so much like to have company." I smiled at him as sweetly as I was able. The young fellow was evidently more than half convinced that he had made a conquest, while I was quite sure that I had.

When the lieutenant left, the soldiers began to crowd about the windows of the car, staring at me and using abusive language. At length, provoked beyond measure, I called to a major and said to him, "I would thank you, sir, to do something to stop the men from insulting me. I am travelling under a pass from the colonel, and he promised me that I should not be annoyed in this manner."

The major promptly came forward and, pushing some of the soldiers away, said, "Men, keep quiet and do not insult this lady She is on our side. She is Union."

It struck me, as the major was making this little speech, that the soldiers were wiser than some of their officers, although I did not feel any more amiable towards them on that account. I thanked the major for his promptness in coming to my protection and we passed a few words, the idea coming into my head that if I could fall into a conversation with him, I might be able to beguile him into giving me some information worth having. Before we had an opportunity to do more than exchange the ordinary civilities of the day, however, the train began to move and I was unable to improve my acquaintance with him.

Chapter Twenty-One

Human nature is greatly given to confidence, so much so that the most suspicious people are usually the easiest to extract any desired information from, provided you go the right way about it. Women have the reputation of being bad secret-keepers. Well, that depends on circumstances. I have always succeeded in keeping mine, when I have had any worth keeping; and I have always found it more difficult to beguile women than men into telling me what I have wanted to know, when they had the slightest reason to suspect me. The truth seems to be, that while women find it often troublesome and well nigh impossible to keep little secrets, they are first-rate hands at keeping great ones.

For certain kinds of secret service work, women are, out of all comparison, superior to men. One reason for this is that women are quicker-witted and more wide awake than men; they more easily deceive other people, and are less easily imposed upon. As a rule, for an enterprise that requires real finesse, a woman will be likely to accomplish far more than a man.

I was just thinking that my lieutenant had deserted me, when he appeared beside me, having jumped on the rear end of the car as it was starting. He said, "You have no objections to my occupying the same seat with you, have you, madam?"

"I will be greatly pleased if you will go through with me. It has been a long time since I have met any agreeable gentlemen, and I particularly admire officers."

As I said this, I gave him a killing glance and then dropped my eyes as if half-ashamed of having made such a bold advance. The bait took as I expected it would. Giving his mustache a twist and running his hand through his hair, the lieutenant settled himself down in the seat with a most self-satisfied air, and began to make himself as agreeable as he knew how. He had not been seated more than a minute or two before he blurted out, "I guess you're married—ain't you?"

"No, sir. I'm a widow."

"Is that so? Well, now, about how long has the old man been dead?"

"My husband died shortly after the breaking out of the war. I have been a widow for nearly three years."

"Well, that's a pretty good while to be a widow, but I reckon men are scarce down your way. Got any children?"

"No, sir, unfortunately I have no children. Are you married, sir?" I suggested in a rather timid tone, giving him another killing glance.

"No," he replied with considerable force, "but I wouldn't mind being, if I could find a real nice woman who would have me." And with this he gave me a tender look that was very touching.

He then remarked, "I don't believe you will have any difficulty in getting through to Memphis. I will be glad to assist you any way I can." He then said, in a hesitating sort of way, "I hope you won't feel offended if I inquire how your finances are."

"O, no, sir, no offense at all. I am sorry to say that my funds are rather low."

"Well, I'll see you fixed all right until you can hear from your friends." He proceeded to inquire who my relatives were, where they lived, whether they were wealthy or not—he seemed especially anxious on this point—how old I was, whether I had ever thought about getting married again, and so forth. I answered his queries promptly, and perhaps more to his satisfaction than if I had told him the exact truth in every instance.

At length the whistle blew, and the train stopped at his camp. He rushed out without even saying good-bye. While I was wondering where he had left his politeness, I saw him running as fast as he could, and presently dodge into a tent. In a moment or two more, out he came in his shirt sleeves, and ran for the train, with his coat in his hand. He jumped on board just as we were starting. I saw him put on a rather better uniform coat than the out-at-the-elbows blouse he had been wearing, and a paper collar and black necktie. These last I considered as particularly delicate attentions to myself.

He came forward and, seating himself beside me, said, "I will allow myself the pleasure of going through to Memphis with you."

I assured him that I was pleased beyond measure, and came to the conclusion that I would be able to make a most useful ally of him in carrying out my plans for the benefit of the Confederacy.

"Do you see that field over there?" said he, pointing to a good-sized clearing. "That's where our boys had a fight with Forrest."

"Did you run fast?" I asked rather maliciously.

"We had to run. There were too many for us."

"Why," said I, "there seems to be a great many of you."

"O, there's not half enough to do anything. They've got us scattered along this railroad in such a way that it's almost as much as we can do to hold our own, when any kind of a crowd of rebs put in an appearance."

This was interesting, but I did not think it prudent just then to question him any closer on such a delicate subject. He branched off into anecdotes of army life, the fights he had been engaged in, and a variety of matters that do not merit being put on record. At length the train reached Memphis, and my escort requested me to wait on the platform. In a few moments he returned with a carriage and when I was seated in it, he ordered the driver to go to the Hardwick House.

"O, no," said I, "I must go to General Washburn's headquarters first and deliver my despatch and messages."

"I thought you might prefer to arrange your toilet before seeing the general."

"No," I replied. "I must see him immediately, as I was told that this was a matter of great importance. The general won't mind my looks."

The driver was accordingly directed to take us to headquarters, and before many minutes I was ushered into the presence of the provost marshal, to whom I stated my errand. The lieutenant being with me undoubtedly prevented many questions being asked. He put in a word now and then which had the effect of establishing me on a satisfactory footing with the provost marshal. That official, when he had heard my story, said, "Madam, I am sorry, but the general is indisposed and cannot see you."

"O, sir, I must see him. It is impossible for me to communicate what I have to say to anyone else."

"Did the person who confided the paper to you give you any private instructions?"

"Yes, sir, and he was very particular in telling me to communicate with the general in person, and with no one else."

"Well, madam, I am sorry, but the general is unable to see you. You will either have to leave the paper with me, or else call again."

This struck me as a decidedly odd way of doing business. I concluded that if mat-

The Union Lieutenant runs to catch the train.

ters were managed in this style at headquarters, Memphis would not be a difficult place for me to operate in, or for the Confederates to operate against. I knit my brows, looked vexed and perplexed, tapped the ground with my foot, and pretended to be thinking deeply about what course I had better pursue. After a few moments I said, "I promised to see the general himself, but if he won't see me, I will have to write to him."

I sat down and scribbled off a brief note to the general. This note and the despatch I enclosed in the same envelope with a request that it be given to the general immediately.

Chapter Twenty-Two

The next morning the lieutenant made his appearance bright and early, and said he had raised a hundred dollars for me. Expressing my gratitude to my friend, I said that he would place me under still further obligation if he would aid me in obtaining some better clothing than I had on. Taking half the money, he invested a good portion of it in a stylish bonnet, a handsome piece of dress goods, and a pair of shoes. During the day I was called upon by several officers and others, and one lady loaned me a dress to wear until mine should be finished. Thus, I was in a short time fitted out in good style, and was able to figure as I desired in such society as Memphis afforded.

My new friends were extremely anxious to know what was going on within the rebel lines. I endeavored to gratify their curiosity as well as I could, and in return made an effort to find out about the contemplated movement of Federal troops. I did not have a great deal of trouble learning nearly everything about the number and disposition of the troops along the railroad and also that the force at Colliersville was being strengthened in apprehension of an attack. This information I promptly communicated to my confidante, who started for Forrest's headquarters without delay. The concentration of the Federal force at Colliersville, I believe, was induced by the despatch I delivered to General Washburn. It had the effect of leaving a gap in the Federal line for Forrest to step through. When, in a day or two, intelligence was received that he was on a grand raid through western Tennessee, I knew that the plot I had engaged had succeeded in the best manner.

While attending church on the Sunday following, I noticed in the congregation a Confederate officer in citizen's clothes whom I knew by sight and who belonged to my brother's command. After the service was over, I watched him as he left the church and, seeing him turn the corner, I said to the lieutenant who had accompanied me, "Let us walk down this street." I saw him turn toward the Hardwick House, but on reaching the hotel I found that the man had disappeared. I was resolved to find out what I could about him from some of the servants, and to send him a note requesting a private interview. Fortunately, however, I was not compelled to resort to any such expedient, for, on going in to dinner with the lieutenant, I saw him at one of the tables.

The lieutenant was conducting me to the seat we usually occupied, but I said, "Suppose we go over to this table today. I think we will find it pleasanter." I seated myself next to the Confederate, indicating to the lieutenant to take the seat on the other side of me. When the waiter came to get our orders, I asked him to bring me a couple of cards. On one of the cards I wrote some nonsense, which I sent by the waiter to an officer on the other side of the room. On the other I wrote, "Meet me at my room at half past ten this evening, unobserved. Important." This I dropped on the floor, touching the Confederate officer as

I did so to attract his attention.

At the hour named on the card the Confederate officer came to my room, evidently very much perplexed. I hastened to place him at his ease by explaining matters.

I said, "You will pardon me, sir, but this is Lieutnant B. of Arkansas, is it not? I know you, although you do not know me. I am the sister of Captain Velazquez and I am exceedingly anxious to learn where and how he is."

Lieutenant B.'s face brightened up immediately. He stated that he was very pleased to meet me, but was sorry to tell me that my brother had been captured by the Federals about four months before. This unpleasantness determined me to give up the idea of returning to Mobile, but to go North and visit my brother. I had quite a lengthy conversation with Lieutenant B. about my brother, and about affairs generally, and announced to him my intention of visiting the North and perhaps acting as a secret service agent. He gave me the names of persons in different places who were friends of the Confederacy and advised me to talk with certain parties in Memphis who could give me valuable information.

The next day I began to prepare for my departure. My friend the Federal lieutenant was very cut up when he heard that I intended to leave. I promised to write to him as soon as I arrived in New York and intimated that I might correspond regularly. He in return procured for me a pass and transportation from General Washburn. Off I started, leaving Memphis— where I was liable at any time to be recognized—with little regret.

My first object was to see my brother. He was the only relative I had in the country and I felt very anxious about him. I pushed forward as rapidly as I could until I reached Louisville, Kentucky. I took a room at the Galt House and communicated with a Mr. B., whose name had been given me as one in whom I could confide. I told Mr. B. who I was and what was my errand, informing him that I was short on funds. He said that he would make an effort on my behalf and, accordingly, a gentleman called that evening at my room. He was greatly afraid of being seen with me and before he would leave I had to go out into the hall to see that no one was looking. He posted me very thoroughly about the best method of going to work, not only for procuring the release of my brother, but for picking up information of value to the Confederate authorities. He suggested that I should retire early, and be ready to go by the first train in the morning, and said that he would see that I was provided with funds.

Early the next morning I was awakened by a knock on my door. Someone outside asked if I was going on the early train. I replied that I was and hastened to dress. As I was dressing, I was startled to see a large envelope on the floor, which must either have been pushed under the door or thrown in over the transom during the night. I found in it five hundred dollars in greenbacks, and letters to a couple of persons in Columbus, Ohio.

I got off on the early train, and in due time arrived at Columbus. The next day I called on the general in command, and said that I would very much like to visit that rebel brother of mine. Notwithstanding that he was on the wrong side, I could not help having an affection for him, and was desirous of assisting him in case he should be in need. Having satisfied himself that I was all right, the general gave me the desired permit. With a profusion of thanks I bowed myself out of his presence.

My meeting with my brother was a most affectionate one. I disclosed to him part of my plans, and instructed him on how to talk and act towards me. He was to call me his Union sister and to speak of me as a New Yorker. To effect his release I would go on to

Loreta has an affectionate meeting with her Confederate brother.

Washington, if necessary, and see the president and secretary of war. This, however, I found to be unnecessary, for Governor Brough of Ohio, a hearty and good-natured old gentleman, happened to be at the same hotel with me. He took quite a fancy to me and promised to use his influence to obtain a parole for my brother. In a short time, the prisoner was released and ordered to proceed to General Dix, at New York, the idea being that he was to remain with me in the city. In company with my brother, therefore, I proceeded East and went to New York where I left him, while I went on to Washington for the purpose of seeing what could be done in aiding the Confederate cause at the Federal capital.

Chapter Twenty-Three

At the time of my arrival at the North, the anti-war party was concentrating its strength for the approaching presidential campaign. Many men were confident that the election would place a president in the White House whose policy toward the South would be radically different from Mr. Lincoln's. It was an important part of the duty of Confederate agents at the North to aid the anti-war party. Many officials in the government were either secret service agents of the Confederacy or in the pay of such. In all the large cities were merchants who were growing wealthy by sending goods, arms, and ammunition to the South. I had a good deal to do with these frauds and it may be thought that I was as culpable as those whom I now denounce. It was not pleasant for me to do what I did or to associate with the men I did. There is nothing, however, in this portion of my career that I am ashamed of. I have no hesitation whatever in giving a plain statement of the enterprises in which I engaged during the last eighteen months of the war.

I hoped, on going to Washington, to find someone with whom I was acquainted. On my arrival in the capital I made inquiries concerning the prominent officers in the army there. I was not long in learning that General A. and Captain B. were both on duty in or near Washington. I saw both the general and the captain several times and, in the course of conversation with one of them, he happened to say something about Colonel Baker which excited my interest. I had never heard of this individual before, but I now speedily learned that he was the chief government detective officer, and that he was uncommonly expert in hunting down rebel spies. I immediately concluded that Colonel Baker was a person whom I should become acquainted with at the earliest possible moment, and that it would be advantageous for me to meet him through one of my military friends. The general introduced me to Colonel Baker, and spoke of me in such a manner as to put me in the good graces of this terrible man at the start.

Colonel Lafayette C. Baker occupied at Washington a similar position to that held by General Winder at Richmond, although he scarcely had the large powers and authority of the chief of the Confederate secret service. In fact, Colonel Baker was a detective officer more than anything else, and had comparatively little to do with military matters. His chief employment was to hunt down offenders of all kinds, and he was much more successful in this than he was in procuring information for the war department. He was a tolerably fair-looking man, a returned Californian, and had the bronzed face and wiry frame of a western pioneer. His eyes were a cold gray and had a peculiarly sharp and piercing expression. I came into the presence of so formidable an individual with some degree of trepidation, but

I soon learned to regard him as not half as ferocious as he looked. He was a man who, under some circumstances, I might have taken a genuine liking to. The more I saw of Winder the less I liked him and the more I was afraid of him.

On being introduced to Colonel Baker by General A., I asked if he could give me a position in his detective corps. I expressed myself with considerable bitterness with regard to the rebels and the treatment I professed to have received at their hands. I endeavored to impress upon him that I was quite as anxious to engage in spy duty for the purpose of being revenged on them as for the cash I expected to earn. The colonel, however, was cautious - he would see about it; he would talk further with me; he did not know that he had anything he could give me to do just at present, but he might have need of me shortly, and would let me know when he wanted me, and all that sort of thing.

Having waited about Washington for a week or two without hearing anything from Colonel Baker, I decided to return to New York, as I thought, from a hint in a letter from my brother, that I might be able to commence operations there. I resolved, however, to cultivate Baker's acquaintance at the earliest opportunity, but thought it best not to trouble him again until I had some definite scheme to propose.

When I reached New York and saw my brother, he was expecting every day to be exchanged. He told me that he had been visited by several Confederate agents, who wanted him to carry some documents through when he went South. He was afraid, however, to attempt anything of this kind, and, besides, did not think it would be honorable under the circumstances. I went and saw the agents in question, told them who I was, referred them to people who knew me in the West, and in a general way disclosed to them my schemes for aiding the Confederacy.

They then evinced a great eagerness to have me persuade my brother to carry some despatches through. I said that it would be useless to ask him, and the most I could expect of him was that he would take a verbal message from myself to the officials who knew me in Richmond. It required considerable persuasion to induce my brother to do even this much, but finally, to my great satisfaction, he consented. Shortly after this, my brother went South on an exchange and, in due time, I received information that my message had been delivered, and that I was recognized as a Confederate secret service agent.

In the meanwhile, I made a large number of acquaintances among the adherents of both the Federal and Confederate governments, and did a great deal of work of one kind or another. I visited Washington frequently and always made it a point to see Colonel Baker, to whom I furnished a number of bits of information. The majority were of no particular value to him, although several were of real importance and aided him materially in his efforts to break up certain fraudulent practices, and to bring the rogues to justice. At each succeeding interview, I could see that Baker was becoming more and more favorably impressed with me. I did not doubt that I would finally succeed in securing him as an unconscious ally of myself and my co-workers.

I heard Colonel Baker frequently complain bitterly of the manner in which so many of his neatly laid plans were revealed to the very persons whom he was most anxious should know nothing of them, almost as soon as they were arranged. I endeavored to console him and suggest reasons for the phenomena, but was never able to quite make him understand the mystery. The colonel, as I have before remarked, was not a bad sort of fellow in his way. As I had a sincere regard for him, I am sorry he is not alive now, that he

Loreta confers with Colonel Lafayette Baker.

might be able to read this narrative and so learn how completely he was taken in, and by a woman too. He was a smart man, but not smart enough for all occasions.

Chapter Twenty-Four

A magnificent scheme was on foot during the summer and fall of 1864 for making an attack upon the enemy in the rear which, if it had been carried out with skill and determination, might have given a very different ending to the war. The scheme was no less than an attack upon the country bordering upon the Great Lakes; the release of the Confederate prisoners confined near Sandusky, Ohio and other locations; their organization into an army which was to engage in devastating the country, burning the cities and towns, seizing forts, arsenals, depots and manufacturers of munitions; in fine, of creating such a diversion in their rear as would necessitate the withdrawal of a large force from the front.

In the event of success, the Federal forces would be placed between two fires. The commanders of the Confederate armies in the South and North would be able to crush the enemy and dictate terms of peace, or at least give a new phase to the war by transferring it from the impoverished and desolated South to the rich and fertile North.

While the plan for the proposed attack was maturing, I was asked to attempt a trip to Richmond and consented without hesitation. I was to receive instructions from the Richmond authorities and especially to obtain letters and despatches for Canada. Now was my time to make use of Colonel Baker. Having received my papers and instructions, I went to Washington and called on the colonel. I told him that I had obtained information that a noted Confederate spy had been captured and was now in prison, from whence he could doubtless find means to communicate with Confederates outside. My proposition was that I go to Richmond, and find out exactly who and where this man was, and what he and his confederates were trying to do.

The colonel laughed at my enthusiasm, and said, "Well, you are a plucky little woman. I have half a notion to give you a chance. You must not blame me, however, if you get caught and they take a notion to hang you."

"O," said I, "I don't think my neck was ever made to be fitted in a noose, and I am wiling to risk it."

Colonel Baker finally consented to let me try my luck. I saw very plainly that he did not entirely trust me, or, rather, that he was afraid to trust me too much. I attributed his lack of confidence in me to the fact that I was as yet untried, rather than to any doubt in my mind with regard to my fidelity. I resolved, therefore, to give him such proofs of my abilities, as well as my fidelity, as would insure me his entire confidence in the future.

Baker told me to get ready for my journey immediately. He gave me five thousand dollars in bogus Confederate bills, and one hundred and fifty dollars in greenbacks. I had little difficulty getting through the Federal lines on the passes furnished by Baker. To get through those of the Confederate forces was a more troublesome operation; but when I came to the outposts, I was able to declare my real errand. I was not seriously impeded, and once in Richmond I was, of course, perfectly at home.

I immediately communicated with the authorities, delivered the messages and despatches submitted to me, sent letters to merchants in Wilmington and Savannah, and gave all the information I could about the condition of things in the North. Within a few days I heard, by special messenger, from the parties in Wilmington and Savannah. This man delivered a package to me which was to be taken to Canada, and also orders and sailing directions for certain blockade-runners, and drafts which were to be cashed for the benefit of the Confederate cause.

In consideration of the value of the baggage I was carrying, it was thought to be too great a risk for me to attempt to reach the North by any of the more direct routes. I was consequently compelled to make a long detour by way of Parkersburg, West Virginia. At that place I found General Kelley in command, and from him procured transportation to Baltimore on the strength of my being an attach of Colonel Baker's corps. This was a very satisfactory stroke of business for me, as I was getting short of funds and was, moreover, quite sick. The excitement I had gone through - for this was a more exciting life even than soldiering - and the fatigues of a long and tedious journey had quite used me up.

On arriving in Baltimore, I was so sick that I had to send for a doctor. I offered him my watch for his services, stating that I was detained in Baltimore through the non-arrival of money which I was expecting. He refused to take it and said that I might pay him if I ever was able. The next day I was considerably better, and I continued to improve with rest and quiet. While stopping at Barnum's Hotel, I became acquainted with a young captain in the Federal army. The captain was so affected by my pitiful narrative that he introduced me to General E.B. Tyler, who kindly procured for me a pass to New York.

In New York I was met at the Desbrosses Street ferry by my associate in that city, who had engaged a room for me. He said that he had been getting somewhat anxious for my safety, especially as he was informed that the detectives had received some information of my doings, and were on the watch for me. He himself had seen one of the detctives who were on my track. While I was evidently the person he was after, the description he had of me was a very imperfect one; so that, by the exercise of a little skill, I ought to be able to evade him. To put him on the wrong track, my accomplice had told this detective he thought he knew the person he was searching for, and had procured a photograph of a very different looking woman, and given it to him.

Having cashed my drafts and gotten everything ready, I started for Canada, carrying, in addition to valuable letters, orders and packages, the large sum of eighty-two thousand dollars in my satchel. I was absolutely startled when, on approaching the depot, my companion, pointing to a man in the crowd, said, "That is the fellow to whom I gave the photograph. He is looking for you, so beware of him."

Then, thinking it best we should not be seen together by Mr. Detective, he wished me good luck and said good-bye, leaving me to procure my ticket, and to carry my heavy satchel to the cars myself.

After getting into the cars I lost sight of the detective until the arrival of the train in Rochester, and was congratulating myself that he had remained in New York. At Rochester, however, to my infinite horror, he entered the car where I was and took a seat near me.

When the conductor came through after the train had started, the detective said something to him in a low tone, and showed him a photograph. The conductor shook his head on looking at it, and made a remark that I could not hear. I did, however, hear the detective say, "I'll catch her yet," to which I mentally replied, "Perhaps."

This whispered conversation reassured me a little, as it showed that the officer was keeping his eye open for the original of the photograph, while the woman he was really

The detective shows a photograph to the train conductor.

after was sitting within but a few feet of him. I concluded that I would try and strike up an acquaintance with the gentleman. I thought that perhaps I could say or do something to make him even more bewildered than he was already.

I, therefore, picked up my shawl and satchel and removed to the seat immediately back of him. The window was up, and I made a pretense of not being able to put it down. After a bit, the detective's attention was attracted and he very gallantly came to my assistance. I thanked him with a rather effusive politeness, and he seated himself beside me and and opened a conversation. He did not have the appearance of being a very brilliant genius, but I well knew not to place too much reliance upon outward appearances, especially with members of the detective force.

"You are going to Canada, are you not?" inquired my new-made friend. "Do you live there?"

"O no, sir. I live in England. I am only going to Canada to visit some friends."

The detective now took out of his pocket the photograph which my associate in New York had given him, and handing it to me said, "Did you ever see anybody resembling this? I am after the lady, and would like very much to find her."

"She is very handsome," I replied. "Is she your wife?"—looking him straight in the eyes as I said this.

"Wife! No," said he, apparently disgusted at the suggestion. "She is a rebel spy, and I am trying to catch her. I am on her track now, and I am bound to catch her."

"But perhaps this lady is not a spy, after all. She looks too pretty and nice for anything of that kind. How do you know about her?"

"O, some of our force have been on the track of her for a long time. She has been working for rebel agents here at the North, and has been running through the lines with despatches and goods. She came through from Richmond only a short time ago, and is now on her way to Canada, with a lot of despatches and a big sum of money, which I would like to capture."

"Supposing that this lady is a spy, as you say, how do you know that she has not already reached Canada?"

"Maybe she has," he replied, "but I don't think so. I have got her down pretty fine, and feel tolerably certain of taking her before she gets over the line."

This was a highly edifying and entertaining conversation to me, and I would willingly have prolonged it indefinitely. However, I was afraid to seem too inquisitive, and we dropped into general conversation.

The detective seemed to be determined to be as polite to me as he could. On leaving the cars, he carried my satchel, containing eighty-two thousand dollars belonging to the Confederate government, and a variety of other matters which he would have taken possession of with the utmost pleasure, could he have known what they were. When we passed on board the boat, I took the satchel from him, and thanking him for his attention, proceeded to get out of his sight as expeditiously as I could.

When the customs-house officer examined my luggage, I gave him a wink, and whispered the password I had been instructed to use. He merely turned up the shawl which was on my arm, and went through the form of looking into my satchel.

On my arrival in Canada, I was welcomed with great cordiality by the Confederates there. I distributed my letters and despatches according to instructions; mailed packages for the commanders of the cruisers *Shenandoah* and *Florida*; and then proceeded to the transaction of such other business, commercial as well as political, as I had on hand. There were a number of points about this grand scheme that I would liked to have been informed of, but those who were making arrangements for the raid were so fearful of their plans getting to the ears of the Federals that they were unwilling to tell me and other special agents more than was absolutely necessary for the fulfillment of the duties entrusted to us.

This plan for a grand raid by way of the lakes excited my enthusiam greatly, and I had very strong hopes of its success. Whether the proposed raid would have accomplished all that was expected of it can, of course, never be determined. I, as well as the others, underrated the difficulties of executing such a complex scheme. Be that as it may, something could have been done, more than was done, had everybody been as enthusiastic and determined as myself, and had there been no traitors with us. The scheme failed, when it should have been at least partly successful; but it need not have failed so utterly as it did, had it been managed with wisdom, backed up by true daring.

Chapter Twenty-Five

On my return from Canada, I hurried on to Washington for the purpose of seeing Colonel Baker. I did not know how much information he might have about me by this time, and it seemed like walking into the lion's den. His officers were aware of some of my movements, as they were following me rather too closely for comfort, but whether they had succeeded in identifying the rebel spy with the woman Baker had employed on a confidential mission to Richmond was not clear. It was of such great importance, however, that I gain immediate admittance to the military prisons, that I determined to have the colonel my ally. I more than once fancied what a capital good joke it would be for me, after I had succeeded in getting beyond Colonel Baker's reach, to inform him how badly he had been taken in, and ask him what he thought of my performances from a professional point of view.

While on my way to Washington for the purpose of making a report of my Richmond trip, my prospective interview was anything but a joking matter. The thing had to be done, though; so, stifling my fears, I walked boldly into the colonel's presence, and announced myself as having just got back from Richmond.

Baker received me with proper cordiality, and congratulated me on my safe return. There was nothing whatever in his manner to indicate that he had the slightest suspicion of me. I told him I had obtained the name of the spy whom he was anxious to discover, and such a description of him as would enable me to identify him if I could get to see him. The information I had obtained induced met to believe that he was at Johnson's Island. I then went on to say that it was understood in Richmond that arrangements were being made for a grand stampede of the rebel prisoners.

Baker fell into the trap just as innocently as if he had been a young man from the country, instead of the chief detective officer of a great government. On my suggesting my willingness to follow up by visiting the prisons for the purpose of finding the spy, and if possible discovering any conspiracy that might be on foot, he said he would think about it. I saw plainly that he considered the idea a good one and did not doubt that he would speedily make up his mind to send me.

I proceeded to give him a detailed account of what I saw and heard in Richmond. I then went on to tell him a well-connected story, partly true and partly false, about the way things looked and the way people talked. None of the facts I gave the colonel were of any importance, but they served to give an air of plausibility to my narrative, and to convince him that I was quite an expert spy. I was curious to know exactly how well he was informed with regard to my real movements, and had half a dozen questions on the end of my tongue. I concluded, however, that this would be going too far and might have the effect of exciting suspicions. I did, however, venture to inquire whether he had told anyone that I was attached to the corps.

"No, no," he replied, "certainly not, and I don't want you to tell anyone either. I would rather that even my own people should not know anything about you as a secret service agent."

The next morning, just as I was sitting down to breakfast, the waiter brought me a note from Colonel Baker, in which he stated that he would call to see me about half past ten o'clock. At the appointed time he made his appearance, with a pleasant smile in which there was not a shade of malice or unfriendliness. After making a few unimportant remarks he said, "Well, my little woman, I have made up my mind to let you try your skills as a detective once more, if you are in the same mind you were yesterday."

"Yes," I replied, "I think I can not only find that spy for you, but can discover whether there really is any intention among the rebel prisoners to make a break."

"Try and find out all you can. I want you to make every effort to find him."

"You know, Colonel, I am acquainted with a good many many people down South and I may come upon somebody I know. By representing myself as a disguised Confederate, I may be able to get the prisoners to talk plainer than they would to a stranger."

"If you were to pass yourself off as a Confederate agent and intimate that something was to be done soon to release the prisoners, you might induce them to say whether they have any plans of their own."

"That is about my idea of working; but the only difficulty will be in getting a chance to talk to any of the men privately."

"O, I'll arrange that for you. If those fellows are up to any tricks, I want to know about it at once. There has been talk at different times about the prisoners attempting to stampede. Find out all you possibly can and let me know immediately."

"Well, you can rely on me, and I think you will find me as shrewd as most of your detectives are."

"If you will only keep your eyes and ears well open, and open your mouth only when you have business to talk about, I will most likely find you a good deal shrewder."

"Why, Colonel, you don't appear to have the best opinion in the world of some of your detectives."

"O, they do pretty well, but they are not as smart as they ought to be for the kind of service they are in. Some of my people are after a spy now who has been travelling between Richmond and Canada, but they don't seem to be able to lay their hands on her. If they don't catch her soon, I have half a mind to let you try what you can do, if you succeed well with your present trip."

The conversation was getting rather too personal and I thought it best to change the subject. I asked the colonel when he desired me to start. He said by the first train, if I could get ready. Handing me my confidential letter and two hundred dollars, he shook hands and left, wishing me a pleasant trip and expressing a hope that he would soon receive a good report from me.

When the colonel was gone I laughed heartily at the absurdity of the situation, and wondered with myself whether I would have dared attempt anything of this kind at Richmond with old General Winder. I had no difficulty in concluding that I would have been forced to proceed in a less open, free and easy style about it and congratulated myself heartily that I had so easy a customer to deal with under existing circumstances. Once on board the Western train, I had a long journey before me and plenty of time to think. I planned and schemed until my brain fairly whirled. I was glad to chat a little with some of my neighbors, or to gaze through the windows at the gorgeous scenery that met my eyes at every turn in the road.

At Parkersburg I met General Kelley again. He laughingly suggested that I seemed in as much of a hurry to go West as I had been to go East the last time he saw me. I remarked that in wartimes the enemy had a way of putting in appearances at various points on the compass, and that we had to go for him if we didn't want him to come for us. The general said that if all the generals were as smart about doing what they had to do as I seemed to be, the rebels would have been whipped long ago.

After leaving Cincinnati, en route for Sandusky, I was introduced to a lieutenant who had in charge twenty-seven Confederate prisoners. These he was taking to Sandusky to be placed on Johnson's Island. This officer was a rather flashy young man, who evidently thought he cut a very dashing figure in his uniform, and was given rather more to reflection on his own importance than to the acquisition of useful knowledge. Not knowing what use I might have for him, I tried to be as cordial as possible, and long before we reached Sandusky we were on the best of terms. He permitted me to have a talk with the prisoners, whom I questioned as to what commands they belonged to, when they were captured, and other matters, and gave them each a dollar out of Colonel Baker's money. Several of the more intelligent of them exchanged glances with me, which intimated that they understood that I had a purpose in cultivating the acquaintance of the lieutenant, and was disposed to befriend them by any means in my power.

The lieutenant took such a fancy to me, and was so excessively gallant, that he insisted on paying all my incidental expenses along the road. It was midnight when we reached Sandusky. The Lieutenant put me in the hotel coach and excused himself for a few minutes until he could dispose of his prisoners. We then drove to the hotel, where he procured for me a room. After seeing me safely installed in my quarters, he said goodnight and expressed a hope that he woud have the pleasure of escorting me to breakfast in the morning.

When I awoke the next moring I went to the window and looked out upon the lake, seeing in the distance what I supposed to be Johnson's Island. This little piece of ground, rising off there so serenely and beautifully from the bosom of the lake, was to be the scene of my next great effort in behalf of the Confederacy—an effort that, if crowned with success, would do more to promote success of the cause than all the fighting and campaigning I had done. It was a great responsibility that rested upon me, this preparing the way for the grand attack which was to transfer the seat of war to these beautiful lake shores, to release these prisoners and perhaps to end the war. I trembled to think that by some trifling slip or mistake the whole scheme might miscarry and come to nothing.

When I was dressed, I found my lieutenant waiting to take me in to breakfast. As soon as he was out of sight, I went to the telegraph office and sent despatches to the Confederate agents at Detroit and Buffalo, announcing my arrival, and received their responses. This duty performed, I started for the boat that was to carry me over to the island.

On arriving at the island, I showed my letter from Baker to the commanding officer, and explained to him that I was searching for a rebel spy. I was admitted into the enclosure and permitted to speak freely to the prisoners. My greatest fear now was that some of the Confederates would recognize me, and say or do something and spoil everything. Glancing around the enclosure, however, I could see no signs of recognition on the faces of the prisoners, although a number of them were gazing curiously at me. At length I spied a young officer whom I had known slightly when I was Lieutenant Harry T. Buford, who I knew to be a bright, intelligent fellow. Calling him to me, I asked him a few immaterial questions, until we had walked out of ear-shot of the others.

When we were where no one could overhear us, I said, "I am a Confederate, and have got in here under false colors; I have something important to say to you."

"I hope you have some good news for us."

"Yes, it is good news: it concerns your liberation. It will depend a great deal on yourselves whether anything can be done. If the prisoners will cooperate in the right spirit, at the right moment, with our friends outside, not only will they secure their release, but they will be able to hit the Yankees a staggering blow."

His eyes sparkled at this. I saw that he was eager to engage in any enterprise to secure his liberation. I was only fearful that in his excitement he would do something incautious.

I therefore said, "You must be very careful, keep cool, and don't give a hint as to who I am. I have a despatch here which will tell you what are the arrangements, what the signals outside will be, and what you are to do when you see them. When you are once outside of the prison, you will find plenty to help you."

I then dropped on the ground a package containing eight hundred dollars. He sat down on a block of wood in front of me and commenced whittling a stick, while I stood close to him with my skirts covering the package. When the guard was looking the other way, he seized the package and slipped it into his boot, then went on whittling in as unconcerned a manner as possible. Wishing him good-bye and success, I shook hands with him, passing the despatch as I did so. The precious paper once in his possession, he started off, whistling and whittling as he went, while I hurriedly returned to the office, where I told the commander that I was unable to find the man I was looking for and would have to visit some of the other prison camps.

I now wrote a letter to Colonel Baker in which I stated that the man I was looking for was not at Johnson's Island, and that I would go on to Indianapolis and visit the prison camp there. I went to the telegraph office and sent despatches to the Detroit and Buffalo agents, and one to St. Louis for the agent there to send certain parties to meet me in Indianapolis. The next morning I was off for Indianapolis. I afterward wished that I had remained, for I felt confident that had I been in Sandusky when the time for the blow came, and had been entrusted with the direction of affairs, there would have been no such miserable fizzle as actually did occur.

Loreta talks with a captured Confederate officer at Johnson's Island.

Chapter Twenty-Six

On my arrival at Indianapolis, I found two men from St. Louis awaiting me. I had a long talk with them about the condition of affairs, and delivered the despatches I had for them. One of them was to go to the borders, to operate with the Indians; the other was to report to Quantrell on some secret business. I was now to wait in Indianapolis and occupy my time in obtaining access to the prison camp. Exactly how to get into the enclosure was something of a problem as, for a number of reasons, I was desirous of doing this without figuring as Colonel Baker's agent. Where there is a will there is a way, and I speedily found a very easy way to accomplish my object.

Walking towards the prison camp the day after my arrival, I met a cake-woman who, I surmised, was permitted to go among the prisoners and trade with them. Going up to her, I purchased a few cakes and said, "Why, do you go into the prison, among those dirty rebels?"

"Yes; the officers all know me and the seargent always looks through my basket to see that I haven't anything contraband."

"Do you think they would let me in with you?"

"Yes. Come along with me; I'll get you in."

When we came to the gate, while the sergeant was examining her basket, the old woman said, "Sergeant, this is my sister. She came to see the rebels. She never saw one."

The sergeant laughed, and passed us both in without further parley. The cake-woman soon had a crowd of men around her investing their cash in the contents of her basket. I spied a major whom I had met in Richmond, but who had never seen me in female attire. Going up to him, I had a hurried conversation, in a low voice. I told him that now was the time for the prisoners to make a break, as there were no troops at hand worth speaking of. I told him what was being done elsewhere, and suggested that they should try and reach the southern part of the state. I then gave him some money and hurriedly left him to rejoin the old cake-woman, whose basket was by this time emptied, and who was prepared to leave.

I wrote a letter to Colonel Baker informing him that the man I was looking for was not at the Indianapolis camp, but that I had information which led me to think I would find him at Alton. If he was not there, I would give the whole thing up and return East.

I had no intention of going to Alton. Being under obligation to remain for some time in Indianapolis, I was desirous of employing myself to the best advantage. I resolved to go to Governor Morton to obtain a clerkship, or some position which would afford me facilities for gaining information. He said there was nothing he could do for me, but that I might be able to obtain employment at the arsenal. This, it struck me, was a most capital idea, to see what I could do where they were manufacturing munitions to be used against my Confederate friends. At the appointed time, I appeared at the arsenal and was sent into the packing-room, where I was instructed in the mystery of packing cartridges.

Immediately upon Governor Morton's suggesting that I obtain employment at the arsenal, the idea of blowing up that establishment entered my mind. After going to work, I soon perceived that this was possible without much risk to myself, provided I took proper precautions. I found, however, that I would not be able to blow up the arsenal without destroying a number of lives and I shrank from doing this. There was a wide difference between killing people in a fair fight and slaughtering them in this fashion. To get myself

A Union sergeant examines the cake-woman's basket.

out of the way of a temptation that was constantly growing stronger and stronger, I suddenly left, after having been at work about two weeks.

I was anxious to leave Indianapolis, but was unable to move for lack of orders and cash. Finally, I received orders by telegraph to proceed to Cairo. I found, on reaching that place, letters which directed me to go to St. Louis, and to stop at the Planters' House to see if I could find out about the projected Federal movements from the officers who were making it their headquarters. I judged that I would not be able to do much by going as a guest, which would also have been inconvenient as it would have necessitated a different kind of clothing from that which I was then wearing (I was figuring as a widow woman in greatly reduced circumstances). It occurred to me that the best plan was to obtain a situation at the Planters' House as a chambermaid. I took lodging at a private house for a few days, until I could mature my plans.

On applying for employment as a chambermaid, I was told that there was no vacancy and that there was not likely to be any. This rather nonplussed me, and I was unable to determine what device to adopt next. I tried a number of ways to find out what I wanted to know, but was entirely unsuccessful. My only chance, therefore, seemed to be to gain access to the officers' quarters when they were out; and to the accomplishment of this I put my wits to work.

I struck up a sort of acquaintance with one of the chambermaids who seemed disposed to be quite friendly. I was not long in becoming intimate with her; and, as I made her a number of little presents, and displayed a marked liking for her, she speedily took a great fancy to me. I called upon her one evening and invited her to go out with me. While she was dressing I slipped her pass key in my pocket. In the morning, missing her key, she began an industrious search for it. I heard her ask one of the other girls to lend her a key, saying that she had lost hers.

As soon as she was out of the way, and when I thought that the officers whose rooms I wished to visit were likely to be away, I slipped downstairs to execute my dangerous errand. Luckily, I met no one and contrived to get into three rooms, where I read a number of despatches and orders, one or two of which were of some importance, but did not succeed in discovering what I was chiefly in search of. On coming out of the third room, I came very near being caught by a bell boy who turned into the corridor just as I had finished locking the door. Putting on a sort of bewildered look, I said in an innocent sort of way, "Which is the servants' staircase? I think I must have got into the wrong hall."

The boy was not particularly bright and I made off as fast as I could. On reaching my lodgings, I wrote out the information I had obtained and forwarded it to the proper agent. In reply to this note, I received a despatch directing me to go to Hannibal, where I would find a package awaiting me. The delivery of this despatch was the last transaction of the western trip which I made under the auspices of Colonel Baker. Not more than a day or two afterwards, I learned of the failure of the attempt to release the Johnson's Island prisoners, and consequently of the grand scheme I had been laboring to promote.

I did not know who was to blame for this failure, but I felt that if all the rest had done their duty as efficiently as I had done mine, success would have crowned our efforts. I resolved to return East, and dissolve all connections with my late co-workers, and to have nothing more to do with schemes that would require confederates in the future. I was beyond measure indignant when I learned, as I did before I reached Philadelphia, that the whole thing had fallen through owing to the blundering cowardice and treachery of one individual The agent whom I met at Philadelphia persuaded me that there was no use in getting discouraged by this misadventure and that there was still plenty of important work for the Confederacy to be done.

I was so decidedly unwilling to engage in any similar enterprise, at least just then, that it was proposed that I attempt something in the blockade-running line. The proposition looked feasible; and, allowing myself to be persuaded, I wrote a letter to Colonel Baker, resigning from the secret service, under the plea that I had obtained other employment of a more remunerative and more congenial character.

Chapter Twenty-Seven

There were numerous manufacturers, merchants, jobbers, brokers and others who were eager to make money wherever it could be made, and whose only object in concealing their transactions, so far as the Southern market was concerned, was to avoid getting into trouble. With such as these, I and my associates found it easy to deal. The first thing done was the chartering of a schooner and the engaging of a warehouse. In this warehouse our goods were stored until we were ready to load. The watchman was perfectly aware that we were engaging in contraband traffic, but he was paid handsomely for holding his tongue. When everything was ready, the schooner sailed for Havana with a regular clearance, one of my associates making matters all right at the custom-house.

It was a troublesome matter getting our cargo together but finally, after many anxious days and nights, during which we expected every moment to be pounced upon by the Federal authorities, our schooner was loaded with wines, drugs, boots, shoes, buttons and military goods. I also purchased a handsome sword and belt and a fine pair of pistols through a sergeant stationed at Governor's Island, who proved useful to me afterward in a variety of transactions.

Everything being ready, the schooner set sail, and succeeded in reaching her port without being overhauled. As soon as she was off, I prepared to start by the steamer for Havana, having orders for coffee and other supplies from Europe and New York for the Confederate agent there. In Havana I found a number of my old acquaintances, who were as busily engaged as ever in running the blockade, although the dangers of the business gave them much discomfort. Blockade-running was a very paying business and what gave these people the most uneasiness was a prospect that the war would speedily come to an end. Their total indifference to the fate of the Confederacy, exccept so far as it affected their opportunities for money-making, had the effect of reviving my enthusiasm, and of making me more than ever resolved to labor for the success of the cause while a glimmer of hope remained.

Having transacted my business in Havana, I went to St. Thomas, where I succeeded in contracting a loan with a Belgian firm on account of the Confederate agents in Canada. This being done, I returned to New York by steamer.

On my return to New York, I was induced to interest myself in the business of reducing the strength of the Federal armies in the field, by preventing the re-enforcements demanded by the government from reaching the front. The services rendered the Confederacy by substitute-brokers and bounty-jumpers cannot be overestimated. Large armies

Loreta and a blockade-Runner in Havana

existed on paper, but while the generals kept calling for more men, they failed to receive them in such numbers as were requisite for keeping their ranks full. The recruiting system adopted by the government was far better calculated for giving abundant employment to rogues of the worst class than it was for keeping the strength of the army up to the proper standard.

Bad as they were, however, the substitute-brokers and bounty-jumpers were not the worst villains of the period. The treasury department itself—where the Federal currency and the bonds upon which was raised money to carry on the contest were manufactured—was the headquarters of a gang of thieves and counterfeiters. A large portion of the funds used in purchasing substitutes, and in carrying on bounty-jumping frauds, was furnished by Confederate agents directly or indirectly from the United States treasury. When I found out that not only were counterfeit Confederate bonds and notes freely manufactured in the North, but that Federal officials made use of this bogus Confederate paper whenever they found it convenient, I had no hesitation in coming to the conclusion that we had the same right to raid the Federal treasury and to injure the Federal credit.

It was Colonel Baker who decided me to go into this business. He seemed to regard it as quite a proper way of fighting rebels to put as many counterfeit Confederate notes as possible into circulation. I was not long in deciding that we rebels had a right to make the thing even by circulating as many bogus United States notes and bonds as we could.

Baker's vigilance having been disarmed, I went to a clerk in the Treasury Department and asked him to assist me in gaining access to the private rooms of the printing bureau, where Federal bonds and currency were manufactued. This clerk was a Confederate sympathizer and a very efficient spy. He gave me a letter of introduction to a man occupying a very high and responsible position. I was told that I might speak with perfect freedom to him with regard to the business I had in hand.

I accordingly went to this official and presented the letter, wondering what he would say and do when he read it. He turned as pale as a sheet, then red, while he trembled so much that I was afraid some of the people in the room would notice it. He finally said a few commonplace things which were intended for the ears of those around us rather than mine, and then requested me to give him my address.

That evening he called on me at my hotel, and I told him, plump and plain, that I and my associates had full information with regard to what was being done in certain of the treasurey bureaux and that we had it in our power to set the detectives to work in such a way that all those engaged in swindling the government would be arrested and brought to punishment. Instead of doing anything of this kind, however, we proposed to share the profits of such fraudulent transactions as were going on in the treasury department.

My friend saw that I "had him," to use a slang phrase that expresses the situation exactly. He agreed to furnish any capital needed to commence operations, or to do any preliminary bribing that was necessary for our purposes. My friend said that he would give me a note which would obtain for me the freedom of the treasury building. He then took his leave and I had little to do with him afterwards, his share of the profits being paid to him by someone else.

My arrangement was that, in the event of my being able to make a satisfactory bargain with officials in the treasury department, I was to be the receiver and bearer of whatever they might confide to my care in the way of bonds, notes, bogus plates and other matters, and was to travel to and fro between Washington, Philadelphia and New York as a confidential manager, while brokers in the two last-named cities were to do the financiering.

The day after receiving the note, I took it to the person in the printer's bureau to whom it was addressed. He proceeded to business at once, requesting me to call the next day at his office when, he said, the matter would be arranged to my satisfaction. I called at his office at the appointed hour, and was referred by him to one of his subordinates. With this man I made an arrangement for a conference under a certain cedar tree in the eastern part of the Smithsonian Institution grounds, at nine o'clock in the evening.

Some time before the appointed hour, I strolled into the grounds of the Smithsonian and after finding the cedar tree, hid myself in some bushes nearby, for it occcured to me that these people might take a notion to have me put out of the way. (My apprehensions were groundless, for I had approached them in such a manner that they were compelled to trust me, whether they wanted to or not.) Ere a great while, I heard footsteps approaching, and presently someone coughed in a significant manner, which I interpreted as a signal for me. Having assured myself that he was alone, I went up to him and said, "Good evening." We then sat down together on the grass to arrange our plans.

The scheme I had to propose was quite a modest one. I, as receiver and bearer for certain other parties, should be given electrotype duplicates of bond and currency plates manufactured in the treasury department. For them we would either pay so much, or would share in the profits.

My new acquaintance, however, was in favor of going into business on a grand scale. He proposed using government money and bonds for speculative purposes and floating bogus bonds—both Federal and Confederate—upon the English market. He was to manage the matter in the treasury department, I was to act as go-between, and certain brokers in Philadelphia and New York were to attend to the outside business. We parted with the understanding that we were not to meet again until I was ready to report the result of our operations, and hand him his share of the profits.

The next day a plate was delivered to me which I immediately put in my trunk. Subsequently I received a note informing me that I would find a package under the cedar tree in the Smithsonian grounds. The package, which on examination was found to contain fifty-five thousand dollars' worth of government paper, was waiting for me, covered with loose leaves to screen it from any casual passerby. Securing my booty, I returned to the hotel, rang the bell for my bill, and started for Philadelphia.

On reaching Philadelphia, I bought a large amount of bogus Confederate bonds. I then went to New York where we went to work to turn the money belonging to Uncle Sam over and over as rapidly as we could, making it pay us a handsome profit each turn.

After we had been operating six days with the money from the treasury, I telegraphed to my confederate in Washington, stating how much had been made and asking whether I should keep on. The reply was to keep going for ten days longer and return to Washington in time for the monthly reports to be made out.

I continued to take an active part in such transactions for several months, travelling between Washington, Philadelphia and New York, and often having about me immense sums of money. At length, however, I became afraid to risk it any longer, as Colonel Baker had commenced investigations in the treasury department, and went out of the business of money-making for the time being. I did the fair thing by the treasury people in giving them a hint with regard to Baker, and then made haste to get out of the way until the storm should blow over.

The bounty-jumping and substitute-brokerage frauds arose out of a contest between the efforts of the Federal government to maintain the armies on the field at their maximum strength, and the determination of nearly the entire body of male citizens to escape military duty by any means in their power.

Under the conscription law, persons drafted were permitted to furnish substitutes if they could get them, and the purchasing of substitutes became an important branch of industry, in which immense sums of money were made. Anything like volunteering, in a proper sense, had ceased long before, but each locality, being anxious to avoid the conscription, made desperate efforts to fill its quota of men by offering bounties to encourage enlistments. The payment of these bounties was a direct encouragement to desertion. Bounty-jumping or escaping from the recruiting officers and enlisting all over again was carried on all over the country.

The rates which were paid for substitutes varied from five hundred to twenty-one hundred dollars. The parties with whom I was associated enlisted chiefly for the army, and did very little for the navy. The bulk of our profits, so fast as they were made, went to Canada or England, and some of the parties who received the money are today living in luxury on it. It was a matter of constant surprise to me that some effort was not being made by the government to put a stop to the outrageous frauds that were being committed in the most open manner every day.

The matter finally was taken in hand by Colonel Baker, who came to New York for an investigation. He kept himself very quiet to prevent those against whom he was operating from knowing knowing that he was in the city until he was ready to deal with them. When I recieived a "strictly private and confidential" note from him, requesting me to call on him at seven o'clock at the Astor House, I scarcely knew what to make of it. Fearful that something against me had been discovered, I was in considerable doubt as to whether to respond or not. My previous experience with Baker, however, had taught me that the bold way was much the best way, and so I concluded to see him at the hour mentioned, for the purpose of finding out what it was he wanted of me.

I accordingly went to the Astor House, and sent up my name. The colonel met me in the parlor and said, with a smile, "Now tell me, my good woman, what have you been doing with yourself?"

"O, I have been visiting my relations."

"I received your letter," continued the colonel, "but I have been surprised at not seeing you in Washington since your return from the West."

" I didn't go to Washington, because I really didn't care to see you. I made such a bad failure on that trip that I was ashamed of myself."

Baker took a good-natured view of what he called my bad luck and went on to tell me what his errand in New York was, and to ask me to aid him in certain matters.

I professed to know little about the bounty and substitute frauds, but consented to try and find out what he wanted. The first thing I did after parting with Baker was to warn my associates, so that they might close out before it was too late. What became of the others in the business I did not care, and was rather glad than otherwise to have an opportunity of putting Baker on their track. In a couple of days I furnished the colonel with the

A bounty-jumper views a poster offering bounties.

information he wanted, and before a great while, the whole bounty-jumping fraternity were thrown into consternation by his raid upon them. But before he had more than fairly gotten under way with his work, the assassination of Mr. Lincoln occurred, and he was recalled to Washington to search for Booth and his companions.

Chapter Twenty-Eight

Shortly after my withdrawal from the bounty and substitute brokerage business, I was requested to make a journey to the West, for the purpose of procuring some information which my associates deemed of importance.

My first stopping-place was Dayton, Ohio. There I dressed myself as a poor girl, and began to look for a situation to do housework. I was not very long in obtaining a situation in a family of Union proclivities. By listening to the conversation in the family, I discovered that there were a number of "Copperheads" in the city, and learned the names of some of the most prominent of them. I also picked up much other useful information that might otherwise have been unattainable.

Before I had been in the house three days, the bad temper of its mistress got the better of me and I resolved to leave. I was soon on my way to Columbus, where I made some inquiries with regard to prisoners, but before I could make any definite arrangements, I received a telegraphic despatch directing me to go to Canada. Proceeding as rapidly as I could to Canada, I had a conference with the agent there and then hastened to New York. I went to see the broker with whom I was in partnership and found him considerably exercised. I allowed myself to be persuaded into making a trip to London for a personal interview with our agent there, to persuade him to sell off the paper we held at any cost.

I accordingly proceeded to London by the next steamer, and was soon plunged into business. Confederate bonds were not selling very well at that time, but as ours cost us very little, we could afford to dispose of them at very moderate figures and still make a handsome profit. I did not think that the end was as near as many persons supposed, but saw very clearly that there was no market in London just then for Confederate bonds. Congratulating myself that I had made out as well as I had, I posted to Liverpool and arrived there just in time to catch a steamer.

As we were going into New York harbor we heard the news of Lee's surrender, which had taken place the day before. Many of the passengers seemed to think that this was practically the winding up of the war. I could not bring myself to believe this. I resolved to stick by my colors to the last, and to labor for the Confederacy so long as a shadow of hope remained.

Having professed an eager desire to work for the cause so long as there was a cause to work for, my associates suggested that I should proceed immediately to Missouri with despatches for Quantrill. I accepted this mission without hesitation and was soon speeding westward. I did not get as far as Quantrill's headquarters, as I was lucky enough to meet one of his couriers, to whom I delivered the despatches.

Having discharged this errand, I went to Columbus, Ohio, where I took rooms at the Neil House. I was soon asleep, but could not have been so very long, before I was awakened by the continual buzzing of the telegraph wires, which were attached to the corner of the hotel. I paid little attention to this noise and dozed off again. A second time I was

News of Lee's surrender is received in New York Harbor.

awakened by it and began to conjecture what could be the matter. I was too tired to make any inquiry just then. I dropped off into a sound sleep and did not awaken until morning.

I arose quite early and, going to the window, saw that the whole front of the building was draped in mourning. A great number of people were moving about the hotel, and a considerable crowd was already assembled in the hall. I asked a gentleman whom I met hurrying downstairs what was the news, and he told me that President Lincoln had been assassinated by one J. Wilkes Booth the night before!

This intelligence startled me greatly, both on account of the terrible crime itself, and because I felt it could work nothing but harm to the South. I also felt for Mr. Lincoln and his family; for I liked him, and believed that he was an honest and kind-hearted man, who tried to do his duty, as he understood it, and was well disposed toward the South.

This sad event rendered it necessary that I have an immediate conference with my associates in the East. I returned as fast as I could to New York, and from thence on to Washington. I was requested to make a trip west again, for the purpose of communicating with certain parties, and accordingly departed on my last errand on behalf of the Confederacy. My business being transacted, I started to return, and again found it necessary to pass through Columbus. When I arrived there the body of Mr. Lincoln was lying in state. I doubt if the little city ever had so many people in it before. All day long a stream of men and women poured in at one door and out at the other of the apartment in which the casket containing the remains of the president was lying. It was a sad sight and it troubled me greatly—so greatly that I was scarcely able to eat or sleep. In addition to my natural grief, I could not prevent my mind from brooding on the detrimental effects which the assassination would have on the fortunes of the South.

The next morning, I returned to Washington and called to see Colonel Baker. Baker said that he had an engagement but would see me at half past seven at my hotel. That evening he came in with a friend of his from Baltimore. As we seated ourselves, Baker said to his friend, "This is one of the best little detectives in the country, but unfortunately she does not like the business."

"O, the business does well enough," I replied; "but I don't like having bad luck in it.

"We can't always have good luck, you know," said Baker. "But I have a job on hand now I think you can manage. I want you to find this woman who is travelling as a Confederate agent. Some of my people have been on her track for a long time, but she is a slippery customer, and they have never been able to lay their hands on her."

I knew it was myself Baker meant, especially when he took out a picture similar to the one the detective had shown me a number of months previous. What could make him so eager to capture me just at this particular moment? Could he possibly suspect me of having anything to do with the assassination plot? The very idea of such a thing made me sick. I managed, however, to maintain my composure, but inwardly resolved that the best thing I could do would be to leave the country at the earliest possible moment.

The colonel and his friend then left. I was to have until nine the next morning to decide whether I would undertake the business he desired me to or not.

When he called to hear my decision, I told him I would do what he desired. He gave me my instructions and I was astonished to find out how much he knew of my movements. He and his men must have been on the point of capturing me many times. They undoubtedly would have done so, had I not the wit to take the course I did in cultivating his acquaintance. With many self-congratulations at escaping thus far, and resolved that Baker should not know me except as one of his own agents, I started for New York, on a search for myself ostensibly, but in reality to wait anxiously for the coming of my brother, in whose company I proposed to get beyond the reach of the detective corps, with all the expedition I could manage.

It was not many days before my brother arrived with his wife, two children, and a nurse. Our arrangements were soon made, and we left New York on one of the Cunard steamers. I wondered what my friend Colonel Baker would think of my disappearance, and could not help laughing at the neat trick I had played upon him.

All of the bright dreams of four years ago had vanished into nothingness, and yet I could not regret having played the part I did. I loved the South and its people with a greater intensity than ever, while at the same time many of my prejudices against the North had been beaten down by my intercourse with its people. There were good and bad in both sections, and I believed that if the good men and women, both North and South, would now earnestly and patriotically unite in an endeavor to carry out the ideas of the founders of the government, they would be able to raise the nation to a pitch of greatness such as had yet been scarcely imagined.